AFFIRMATIONS FOR ARTISTS

Other books by Eric Maisel

Fiction

The Black Narc

The Kingston Papers

Dismay

The Blackbirds of Mulhouse

The Fretful Dancer

Nonfiction

Fearless Creating

Staying Sane in the Arts

Artists Speak (editor)

A Life in the Arts

AFFIRMATIONS

FOR

ARTISTS

ERIC MAISEL, PH.D.

Jeremy P. Tarcher/Putnam
a member of
Penguin Putnam Inc.
New York

Most Tarcher/Putnam books are available at special quantity discounts for bulk purchases for sales promotions, premiums, fund-raising, and educational needs. Special books or book excerpts also can be created to fit specific needs.
For details, write Putnam
Special Markets 375 Hudson Street,
New York, NY 10014

Jeremy P. Tarcher/Putnam
a member of
Penguin Putnam Inc.
375 Hudson Street
New York, NY 10014
www.penguinputnam.com

Published simultaneously in Canada

Library of Congress Cataloging-in-Publication Data

Maisel, Eric, date.
Affirmations for artists / Eric Maisel.
p. cm.
"A Jeremy P. Tarcher/Putnam book."
Includes index.
ISBN 0-87477-839-5
1. Artists—Quotations, maxims, etc. 2. Creation (Literary, artistic, etc.)
3. Affirmations. 4. Conduct of life. I. Title.
PN6084.A8M35 1996 96-13079 CIP
700—dc20

Book design by Judith Stagnitto Abbate

Cover design © 1996 by Tom McKeveny
Cover painting: Piet Mondrian, *Diagonal Composition*, 1921.
The Art Institute of Chicago, Gift of Edgar Kaufmann, Jr. Photograph © 1996 The Art Institute of Chicago, © 1996 Mondrian Estate/Holtzman Trust, Essex, Connecticut

Printed in the United States of America
10
This book is printed on acid-free paper. ♾

FOR ANN

Introduction

I hope that the descriptions of artists' issues and the affirmations that this book contains will help you become a stauncher, wiser, and more loving friend to your own creative nature.

If we wanted to name a single thing that we have learned from a hundred years of clinical psychology, it would be that people, in the course of being raised and growing up, become much more unfriendly toward themselves than we had ever imagined. We have come to call this self-unfriendliness "negative self-talk," "self-sabotaging behaviors," "lack of self-confidence," "low self-esteem," and even, in the language of one psychoanalyst, "psychic masochism."

Artists, who provide us with products of inestimable value, manifest this self-unfriendliness more often than do others. They do work that is difficult and often fails, they compete in a marketplace that provides few of them with a living wage, and at the level of personality, they are sensitive, thoughtful individuals who see the flaws in their own nature and problems in the world. The result is that artists "do not feel okay" about themselves in persistent and abiding ways.

What might an artist do to change this picture? The single most important thing is that she begin to speak to herself in a more positive manner. One of the better ways to become more self-friendly is simply to speak to oneself lovingly and encouragingly.

Since artists are born skeptics, it may be hard for you, the artist-reader of this book, not to snicker a little. But please understand that

I am not advocating simple-minded or saccharine positive thinking. I believe in affirmations, in the complex, rounded way that I have constructed them, for the following reason: If my job is to create myself, it must also be part of my job to encourage myself as I proceed with the arduous, ongoing, never-ending work of self-creation. It is in this sense that I affirm myself and ask you to affirm yourself: as participants in the human drama with tasks to perform and a destiny to fulfill.

To affirm means more than speaking in a friendly way to oneself. To affirm is to declare positively, solemnly, and formally that one is equal to a challenge or is growing equal to that challenge, that one is on a certain track, that one is consciously and forcefully attempting to better oneself and grow in a certain direction. An affirmation can demand that you do a hard thing, acknowledge a profound difficulty, and do more than you have previously done. Being self-friendly is not the same as being easy on oneself.

Nor are affirmations bound up in rules. They need have no religious or spiritual overtones; there are no wrong ways to construct them. "I am not ruined," for instance, is a perfectly fine affirmation, even though it contains a negative. An affirmation can be long or short, poetic or plain. The affirmation arrived at by a client who works with me in psychotherapy is always idiosyncratic and a little unexpected. Each person creates personal affirmations.

Here is one that I like for myself: "All right." "All right" means something like "All right, I don't know what to do next but I do know that I won't turn on the TV or flee from the work." "All right" means "I am going to boot up the computer even though I don't want to." "All right" means "Get ready, body, get ready, mind, get ready, heart, we're staying right here."

If you love a phrase and find that it helps you, that is a valid affirmation. Such affirmations "make firm" something that may not yet be true; they root you in the present moment; and they possess the virtues of simplicity and memorability. *Any* phrase is an affirmation, if it feels self-affirming to you. That is the ball upon which to keep your eye.

Please take time to think about the descriptions of issues and the affirmations that I've provided in this book. An index at the back of the book groups the issues together: if you want to focus on "career," "relationships," "achieving balance," "an artist's happiness," or one of the other ten subjects covered, the index will point you to the related topics. Once you have a sense of the issues you want to focus on, you will want to make use of the affirmations I provide or the ones you devise. The best way to make use of them is to attempt to memorize them, because in the attempt you are reminding yourself over and over again what it is you hope to achieve. Post them up around you and read them aloud as you encounter them during the day: you can take them down when guests come, or you can leave them up and throw affirmation parties.

Affirmations need to be *used* if they are to become incorporated into the fabric of your being. Tape-record them and listen to them. Speak them as you walk, jog, or drive. Send yourself several in a singing telegram. Leave yourself e-mail affirmations. Fax a page of affirmations from your office to your home. Keep them alive and visible. How much do you have to think about pouring yourself that first cup of coffee in the morning? That little should you have to think about using your battalion of affirmations, once you've created them and learned them.

That is your goal, that the affirmations you create become hardwired into your system. When the rejection letter appears in the mail, your affirmation is ready. When a mistake consumes the whole middle of your canvas, your affirmation is ready. When you grow too manic, when a new relationship falters, when you grow too anxious, when you are met by a boulder-sized creative block, your affirmation is ready. It is not that you look for it or try to remember it. It simply arrives, a blessed reflex.

Each of the two hundred issues I describe represents a complex, nuanced set of ideas. The affirmations, too, are longer than ones you may be accustomed to seeing. To make them more useful, you may want to create short affirmations from my longer ones. Let's say, for example, that the issue of "will" is of interest to you. Perhaps your inability to really exert your "will" has been perplexing you; you wake up wanting to write, paint, or compose but discover that you haven't sufficient "willpower" to proceed.

As you think about the complicated matter of "will," as you meditate on it, open to it, and consider the description and affirmation I provide, phrases with the power to serve as your personal affirmations are likely to arise in you. They might sound like any of the following:

- "I *can* exert my will."
- "I will be disciplined."

- "I am increasing my willpower every day."
- "I will!"
- "I can do more today."
- "I am willing!"

These are the sorts of short affirmations you may want to create, ones with real day-in and day-out utility. Please use mine as jumping-off points, not as complete or final answers to the questions you find yourself investigating.

I hope that in the course of encountering this book you will learn how better to affirm yourself, your work, and the world in which you live. Remember that there is nothing syrupy or even inherently optimistic about crafting and using affirmations. It is not optimism that prompts Sisyphus to murmur, "I am free." It is rather a decision he makes, a decision to make firm a certain vision of reality. That decision is made for the sake of the self and, ultimately, for the sake of all humanity.

These, then, are an artist's goals: to work and to affirm the value of that work; to find success and make success; to play a role in the maintenance of culture and to affirm the value of that role; to find love, provide love, and affirm the value of love; and to minimize self-hatred and despair. May this book support you in the realization of these goals.

AFFIRMATIONS

FOR

ARTISTS

Accidents

Many artists are afraid to encourage accidents in their art-making, and in this regard they are like any reasonable person who prefers safety to risk and order to chaos. But this lack of encouragement harms their ability to bring an open mind and an open heart into the studio. To know too soon and too certainly, to control too rigidly, to protect oneself too carefully from making mistakes, to worry too much about wasting watercolor paper, film, or marble, is to create in a state of constipation.

"Every brushstroke has a certain tension, a certain nervousness. Every brushstroke is, in a sense, some kind of an accident."

—Raphael Soyer

"I have discovered that the unasked-for accident can be the salvation of what you are doing."

—Stephen De Staebler

"The nature of the work is to prepare for a good accident."

—Sidney Lumet

"The artist need not know very much; best of all let him work instinctively and paint as naturally as he breathes or walks."

—Emil Nolde

■ *I know that sometimes I so fear making mistakes that I refuse to invite in accidents. But accidents are vital to the work, for they are nothing but my thoughts and feelings organized out of conscious awareness and spontaneously unleashed. Therefore I will control my art less and allow accidents to happen, the unfortunate and the fortunate alike.*

Acting

"Most people pass out of the make-believe stage of childhood, but I'm still in it. I don't think you can act without one foot in the pram."

—**Derek Jacobi**

"The day is lived, and evening comes, and then there's this wonderful time when the lights are lit, and that's when the theater is needed."

—**Joan Littlewood**

"Ultimately the whole show must belong to the actors, who share it with the spectators in two hours of crazed generosity."

—**JoAnn Green**

"Acting is creating with your body and soul."

—**Elizabeth Bracco**

What artist couldn't profit from bringing the skills and personality qualities to her art that actors bring to theirs? To effectively create, an actor must meditate on character, maintain a supple flexibility as he inhabits one role after another, memorize but also improvise, and make strong choices as he brings life to words that, until he throws his soul into them, only rest quietly on the page. The actor's skills and vitality are there for the artist in any discipline to marvel at and emulate.

■ *I will learn what an actor learns: to use my whole being to create art, to give generously of myself in ensemble work, to honor texts while enlivening them, to flesh out with my very own flesh an empathic understanding of other people and other worlds. I, too, am an actor: I recognize and honor my own place on life's stage.*

Addictions

No doubt the artist is something of an addict by nature. She can fall in love with an art form and become addicted to writing, dancing, or sculpting. But if she is addicted to heroin or cocaine, that is another thing entirely. Then she must abruptly stop everything and devote her whole being—not a quarter of herself, not a stray few hours or an afternoon, but her entire being—to not feeding that addiction. She must stop and recover her balance and her freedom: the injunction, if not the way, is simple.

"Any musician who says he is playing better on tea, the needle, or when he is juiced is a plain straight liar."

—**Charlie Parker**

"Quart of whiskey a day for months working hard on a long poem. Wife hiding bottles, myself hiding bottles. Murderous and suicidal. Many hospitalizations, many alibis."

—**John Berryman**

"Drugs were always around."

—**James Taylor**

"While I was an addict, I didn't write anything. I didn't have the attention span or the will."

—**David Crosby**

■ *I know I have it in me to get hooked. I must learn to distinguish between those addictions that harm me and those that don't, and then dispute the destructive ones with all of my being. The destructive ones rob me of time, my health, and my dignity: I will not let that be my destiny! I will save myself from my own bad addictions.*

Aging

"I'm working, but there is so much still to be done! And it frightens me to think of my weight of years. But on we go, without fear or hesitation!"

—**Giacomo Puccini**

"To retire is the beginning of death."

—**Pablo Casals**

"At sixty-three years of age, less a quarter, one still has plans."

—**Colette**

"If you have anything better to be doing when death overtakes you, get to work on that."

—**Epictetus**

It goes against an artist's grain to retire. But whether he retires or not, he will age, and along with the perennial challenges that making and selling art bring, along with the perennial existential challenges of living, come a host of new questions to accompany the arthritis and wrinkles. What work will get done in the remaining time? Has the boat sailed on? Has the artist learned even a small part of what he had hoped to learn? Can he find a little peace in this twilight? Or must he still rush on, restlessly and hungrily, to the very end?

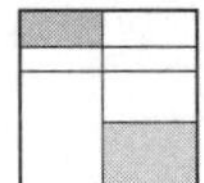

■ *I know that if I am lucky enough to live a while, I will age. Aging simply is. But even as I age I will remain my ideal age inside, old enough to manage my affairs, young enough to work wildly and passionately. I have it in me to fully personalize the phrase "older and wiser."*

Ambition

Even ambition that is pure, that is precisely a hunger for excellence and a commitment to immensity, still comes mixed up with an artist's personality flaws and the natural impurities of the world. With it come envy, greed, and insatiability. With it comes deep disappointment, if someone else gets his role or gallery space. So ambition is vital, but dangerous: it is a keen motive and a driving force, but over what edge can it drive the artist?

"Keep away from people who try to belittle your ambitions. Small people always do that, but the really great make you feel that you, too, can become great."

—**Mark Twain**

"What answer to the meaning of existence should one require beyond the right to exercise one's gifts?"

—**W. H. Auden**

"I will be an artist or nothing!"

—**Eugene O'Neill**

"When you're ambitious, it's really hard to be supportive of other people. But I think it's our job to try, even though one gets jealous."

—**Squeak Carnwath**

■ *I am ambitious. I want; I want so very much! I do not deny my ambitiousness; but I affirm that I will temper it with an appreciation of other things. There is both the mountaintop to aspire to and the patch of plain earth right here to love. I will not put aside my ambitions, but neither will I fail to embrace all the rest that life has to offer.*

Anger

"Alas, we who wished to lay the foundations of kindness could not ourselves be kind."

—**Bertolt Brecht**

"Anger permeates the room. When you walk in with anger, everyone feels it. Lose the anger and you may win the part."

—**Alan Rich**

"Man is a hating rather than a loving animal."

—**Dame Rebecca West**

"Anger is like fire. It burns all clean."

—**Maya Angelou**

It is startling to realize how much ferocious anger each of us harbors. The artist, wishing herself and supposing herself to be peaceable, is herself rocked by anger; and that anger surprises her. She thought she might write of love, but what pours out onto the page is pure vitriol. She thought she might paint philosophically, and what appears on the canvas are torrents of fury. No, the artist is not immune to chronic, even disabling anger: but while she cannot avoid it, she can strive to counterbalance it by really and truly loving.

■ *I acknowledge that I am no stranger to anger and hatred. I have my reasons: but as good as those reasons may be, as many injuries as I've received and as many disappointments as I've experienced, I understand that anger is a pestilence and a blight on my being. I will not befriend my anger; I will not become a hating creature.*

ANXIETY

We have talked about anxiety for a century now and still do not understand its centrality, how it makes or breaks us. Artists, who invite anxiety when they create or perform and who, as alert, sensitive individuals, are susceptible to its vagaries, are obliged to live and deal with persistent anxiety. However, they do not automatically learn from these encounters: that self-education is simply the right choice to make. The ability to survive one's anxiety is, after all, a matter of honest appraisal and subtle transformation.

"I think it true to say that I suffered a nervous breakdown that has lasted a lifetime, though by now I have learned to live with it."

—**Jeanne Reynal**

"Anxiety is the essential condition of intellectual and artistic creation and everything that is finest in human history."

—**Charles Frankel**

"There is no such thing as pure pleasure; some anxiety always goes with it."

—**Ovid**

"If I ignore my work, I start having anxiety attacks."

—**Rosanne Cash**

■ *I know that I must better understand and better manage the anxiety in my life. I accept that the human condition is an anxiety-infested thing, but I do not accept that I must live poorly just because anxiety exists. I will become as cunning as the anxiety that confronts me; when it moves to grip me, I will move to avoid its grip.*

Art Obsessions

"The ideas for stories that thronged my brain would not let me rest till I had got rid of them by writing them."

—**W. Somerset Maugham**

"I wear myself out trying to render the orange trees so that they're not stiff but like those I saw by Botticelli in Florence. It's a dream that won't come true."

—**Berthe Morisot**

"The cypresses are always occupying my thoughts."

—**Vincent van Gogh**

"Wherever I go, I collect sand."

—**Connie Zehr**

"A mind too active is no mind at all."

—**Theodore Roethke**

For artists to obsess about their art is desirable but also troubling. To obsess is to feel pulled about by one's thoughts, agitated, distracted, and separated from other life matters of vital importance. To obsess too virulently is to walk alone in anxiety. But to obsess too little is to wall oneself off from one's own creativity. Maintaining awareness of this distinction is an artist's everlasting duty. Artists must obsess, but they must also manufacture their own shutdown systems, their own ways of giving the brain a rest.

■ *For art to come into existence, it must be obsessed about. Therefore I must cultivate a positive obsessiveness. But obsession is a dangerous necessity. I will monitor my obsessiveness and strive to manage my anxieties: I want to obsess because I am working deeply, not because I am worrying myself to death.*

Artistic Temperament

The artist at her best—wild, passionate, rebellious, and humane—is often too large and truthful a creature for society's taste. The artist at her most outlandish—profane, eccentric, even a little mad—is at least as disquieting a figure. In neither case can she walk the streets with impunity: her grandeur and her strangeness make her a target. Her task is to become a successful eccentric, a strange but wise duck able to venture out of solitary confinement and mingle among society.

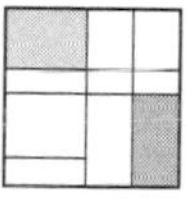

"Perhaps other cities are ready to celebrate the artist and will allow you to get away with more of an artistic temperament, but not a place like Pittsburgh."

—Marie Nugent-Head

"All passions exaggerate: it is because they exaggerate that they are passions."

—Sebastien-Roch Nicolas de Chamfort

"The artistic temperament is a disease which afflicts amateurs."

—G. K. Chesterton

"Art is nature as seen through a temperament."

—Jean-Baptiste-Camille Corot

■ *I will acquire ways of being in the world that serve my purposes. Not everyone need know that I am perfectly willing to tango naked down Main Street or stick my tongue out at the mayor. I will remain a real eccentric, but at the same time I will grow wise in the ways of the world.*

Audience

"How is it that in the so-called barbarian ages art was understood, whereas in our age of progress exactly the opposite is true?"

—**Pierre-Auguste Renoir**

"Since art is dead in the actual life of civilized nations, it has been relegated to these grotesque morgues, museums."

—**Walter Gropius**

"For me, art isn't something you carry up to an East Side Manhattan apartment in an elevator."

—**James Turrell**

"I have had an inordinate and painful concern for the audience in my writing career."

—**Marsha Norman**

An alive piece of art may be more alive than much of its audience, and with this odd truth artists must make peace. An immense wrestling with color in the act of creation is viewed placidly by guests at the apartment of the painting's new owner, the miraculous connection between artist and object having ended. So be it: this predicament may make an artist wonder, it may affect how and what he wants to create in the future, but he must not allow it to addle his brain or ruin his spirits.

■ *I can't control how my work will be received, what will be made of it, or what will be done with it. But it is in my power to chuckle at misunderstandings that arise between my work and its audience. If I can assure no one else's vital connection to art, I can at least assure my own: to the art I create and to all the art that moves me.*

BALANCE

The middle way cannot be achieved by dividing two extremes in half. Balance is not achieved by succumbing to great highs and horrible lows, wild fluctuations in mood and mind, terrible drinking bouts, rages and madnesses, and then surviving to tell the tale. Rather balance is steadfastness in the face of inner and outer turmoil. It is both delicacy and resoluteness; it is the passionate moderation of passion. Balance is no timid, wishy-washy thing: it is the fierce defense of the self's integrity.

"It may seem strange to live in this world of imagery and also to have a normal life. But I sleep like an angel. It is a great privilege to be able to work with, and I suppose work *off*, my feelings through sculpture."

—LOUISE BOURGEOIS

"Wisdom consists in rising superior both to madness and to common sense."

—HENRI-FRÉDÉRIC AMIEL

"Let not the author eat up the man, so that he shall be all balcony and no house."

—RALPH WALDO EMERSON

"In everything the middle road is best."

—PLAUTUS

■ *I have not always aimed for balance in life, but now I see that if I want to realize my dreams I must maintain a fine balance. Imbalance is a waste and a torment; I reject the romantic idea that a candle burning at both ends is to be envied. My aim, as an artist and as a person, is to strike just the right balance.*

Beauty

"When I am working on a problem, I never think about beauty. I think only how to solve the problem. But when I've finished, if the solution isn't beautiful, I know it's wrong."

—**Buckminster Fuller**

"Though we travel the world over to find the beautiful, we must carry it with us or we find it not."

—**Ralph Waldo Emerson**

"Beauty is one of the rare things that do not lead to doubt of God."

—**Jean Anouilh**

"Why should beauty be suspect?"

—**Pierre-Auguste Renoir**

Beauty is rightly suspect. Can't an evil person make a beautiful thing? Can't a beautiful thing be pointless? Can't beauty be manipulated and used for any trivial purpose? And *still* we have the feeling that beauty and truth are intertwined. It is the artist's job to revere beauty without being enchanted by it, to aim for it but also to aim for truth and goodness—just in case they, and not beauty, are the real things of value.

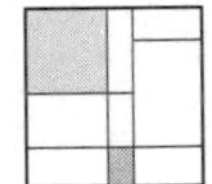

■ *Part of my destiny involves beauty. I will make good, true, and beautiful things just because a sense of the beautiful wells up in me. Beauty brings me joy; and if I must guard against beauty's blandishments, I must also honor the joy it brings. I am built and meant for beauty.*

Blocks

A creative block is the wall we erect to ward off the anxiety we suppose we'll experience if we sit down to work. A creative block is a fear about the future, a guess about the dangers dwelling in the dark computer and the locked studio. A block is a sudden, disheartening doubt about our right to create, about our ability, about our very being. And the cure? A melting surrender, a little love, a little self-love, a little optimism, and a series of baby steps toward the work.

"Blocks produce in the artist an attitude of pessimism and defeat. He loses that necessary touch of arrogance; the drive to produce new things fades; the mind is blunted."

—Lawrence Hatterer

"Something awful happens to a person who grows up as a creative kid and suddenly finds no creative outlet as an adult."

—Judy Blume

"Only let a man say that he will do something and a whole mechanism goes to work to stop him."

—John Steinbeck

"Putting off an easy thing makes it hard, and putting off a hard one makes it impossible."

—George Lorimer

■ *I can't fulfill my destiny as an artist if I remain frightened. I will unblock; I must unblock; and I will do so by loving myself and loving the work. I will raise myself up and move toward the work. I will take a single step in the direction of the studio, and then another. It is my sworn duty to unblock.*

Blue Skies

"The sky is the soul of all scenery. It makes the earth lovely at sunrise and splendid at sunset. In the one it breathes over the earth a crystal-like ether, in the other a liquid gold."

—**Thomas Cole**

"The sky is the source of light in Nature and it governs everything."

—**John Constable**

"I never get tired of the blue sky."

—**Vincent van Gogh**

"Slits in nothingness are not very easy to paint."

—**Georgia O'Keeffe**

The artist—painter or poet, singer or drummer—is a sky worshiper, for the sky's blue immensity mirrors her soul. The child artist looks up at the day sky or the night sky and sees her beautiful dreams reflected there. The adult artist, busy and unsettled, can herself find a moment's peace—and even whole-being rejuvenation—by quietly attuning to a red sky, a gray sky, a black sky, a blue sky. The human race has capital saved in that great vault above us.

■ *I will spend time with the sky, the sun, the moon, the mountains, the ocean waves. I know that I could scorn these loves and turn the sun and moon into nothing: but I find it more heartwarming to affirm them. I am inspired by the blue sky and will not forget where to look for inspiration.*

Boredom

Boredom, disguised in a hundred ways, as misadventures, depressions, and blank evenings in front of the TV, is one of the artist's great nemeses. A director completes his film against great odds—and the day it is done, boredom sets in. The book in progress, so alive to begin with, could now not bore the writer more. Boredom is the thing that regularly arrives between excitements and episodes of meaning: it is as natural as the tides, and in it an artist can drown.

"I'd start to paint a chair, finish an arm, and get bored because I already knew what the other arm was going to look like. But in playwriting you don't know what the second act's going to look like."

—**Anne Commire**

"A subject for a great poet would be God's boredom after the seventh day of Creation."

—**Friedrich Nietzsche**

"Nothing is interesting if you're not interested."

—**Helen MacInness**

"Boredom is a vital problem for the moralist since half the sins of mankind are caused by fear of it."

—**Bertrand Russell**

■ *I hate boredom: it racks my nerves. If I can't maintain meaning every split second, I'll still discourage boredom from visiting by being always ready to make new meaning: by having a "to do" list of fanciful themes and mighty work right at my fingertips. And if boredom still sneaks in, I'll dispute it: I will find an answer to the question of boredom.*

Breadth

"Sometimes I dream of a work of really great breadth, ranging through the whole region of object, meaning, and style. This, I fear, will remain a dream, but it is a good thing to bear the possibility occasionally in mind."

—**Paul Klee**

"Creative experience foreshadows a new Heaven and a new Earth."

—**Nikolai Berdyaev**

"The very freedom and expressiveness we find missing in life we find present in art."

—**Nicholas Wolterstorff**

"Do not set out to make Mexican art, or American, Chinese, or Russian art. Think in terms of universality."

—**Rufino Tamayo**

The artist dreams of works of real breadth; but, limited by his personality and the nature of his medium, limited by inner disturbances and loss of purpose, he often works more narrowly than he'd intended. He then feels the great gulf between the earth-shattering work he had hoped to make and the earthbound work he has fashioned. But he must dry his eyes and look at the song or statue he's fashioned, which may indeed be worthy. The breadth he dreams of is *the* goal; but works that do not rise to that ideal may still have the spark of life in them.

■ *I dream of creating great work and I will never abandon that dream. Such work will have enormous breadth; and I will birth it. But I will honor the good work I manage to do, for the standard of measure is not an imperious ideal but an ideal of human proportions. Whenever I move the spirit even a little, I will feel successful.*

Business

The artist had not intended to use her wits, passion, and vitality in pursuit of the art of the deal, nor had she quite understood how mired she was in a mercantile universe. She would wish it to be otherwise: but it isn't, and she must adapt. Buying and selling define the world she works in: she may chat about goodness and beauty over coffee, but then she must get on the phone and start wheeling. Art and business may be strange bedfellows, but an artist must make room in her bed for both.

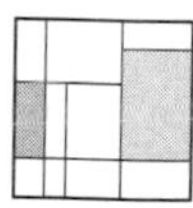

"I think that there is nothing more opposed to poetry, ay, more opposed to life itself, than this incessant business."

—**Henry David Thoreau**

"We sell books, other people sell shoes. What's the difference? Publishing isn't the highest art."

—**Michael Korda**

"There is now scarcely any outlet for energy in this country except business."

—**John Stuart Mill**

"Publishing is an act of commerce."

—**Richard Snyder**

■ *Insofar as it is possible, I will keep art and business in their separate spheres. But I affirm my willingness to dirty my hands in the marketplace. I recognize that here on earth the sacred and the profane must regularly meet, shake hands, and collaborate.*

CALLING

"I don't think you can prevent an artist from being and I don't think you can cause one to be. No one knows what makes an artist."

—**ROBERT ENGMAN**

"I never *wanted* to be a composer. I *am* a composer, which is a different thing."

—**VIVIAN FINE**

"I am in the world only for the purpose of composing."

—**FRANZ SCHUBERT**

"My health may well be better preserved if I exert myself less, but in the end doesn't each person give his life for his calling?"

—**CLARA SCHUMANN**

If an artist is called—if he *must* write, paint, act, or dance—it is very hard for him to assign a positive value to other life pursuits or to tolerate roadblocks that bar his way. It is surely a blessing that meaning attaches to something in his life, that he loves something with all his heart. But a calling that prevents, by its obsessive nature, a person from pursuing other rich avenues, and that provides so very many stern obstacles, must be numbered among life's mixed blessings.

■ *My love affair with art is not an illusion, but the idea that nothing else on earth is worth pursuing may well be. I affirm that even if I am called to be an artist, I will not forget what it means to be a human being, with all the challenges and possibilities that higher calling entails.*

Career

An artist hardly begins his adult life by mapping out the contours of his career. He simply knows too little about himself, his discipline, and the world in which he's embedded to be able to make such calculations. But a time does come, after years in the trenches, when he can begin to fathom what his career has looked like so far and what it will look like if he continues as he's proceeded. When this readiness comes, the artist is likely to find himself exclaiming, "Wow, are there a lot of changes that need making!"

"I never got a job I didn't create for myself."

—Ruth Gordon

"With an apple I will astonish Paris."

—Paul Cézanne

"Write a novel if you must, but think of money as an unlikely accident."

—Pearl Buck

"As a younger man I wrote for eight years without ever earning a nickel, which is a long apprenticeship, but in that time I learned a lot about my trade."

—James Michener

■ *I want to produce a body of work, acquire a reputation, earn money from my art, garner opportunities, and in general have what is called a successful career. I will do all the necessary things, including making changes in the work I do and improving my business skills, to help myself fashion that successful career. I will have the career I've long dreamed of having.*

CHANGE

"I've found that every time I've made a radical change, it's helped me feel buoyant as an artist."

—**DAVID BOWIE**

"You've got to be a fool to want to stop the march of time."

—**PIERRE-AUGUSTE RENOIR**

"Life is a series of collisions with the future."

—**JOSÉ ORTEGA Y GASSET**

"You pour the paint on the snow and take photographs while it melts. All the time it melts, it changes."

—**SARI DIENES**

Embedded in the notion of "change" is the implication that something better can be envisioned, brought into being, and then maintained. It is a supreme challenge for artists to flesh out this fine idea and make it meaningful in their lives. They need, after all, so many things to change: the realities of the art marketplace, the quality of their culture, certain parts of their nature, and much about their circumstances. But still it is the job of each artist to believe in the possibility of meaningful, substantial, and sustainable change.

■ *I am both a conservative and a radical; I would conserve what is valuable but willingly change what requires changing. I affirm the power of change: I am friendly with the idea that some things really need changing. I will contribute to positive change in myself and in the world.*

CHAOS

Chaos is not just motion, mist, and tumult, not just some metaphoric idea found in ancient genesis myths. Chaos is real and feels terrible. It is the sick feeling of not knowing and the scared feeling of present danger, it is the wild, indifferent side of nature that brings hurricanes and religious warfare. This chaos is everywhere—and artists, to fashion art and live truthfully, have no choice but to invite this unwanted guest right into the studio.

"When the individuality of the artist begins to express itself, what the artist gains in the way of liberty he loses in the way of order."

—**PABLO PICASSO**

"When you read and understand a poem, then you master chaos a little."

—**STEPHEN SPENDER**

"Music creates order out of chaos."

—**YEHUDI MENUHIN**

"I try to work all over the canvas at once, because I feel that the forces of nature are unpredictable."

—**NELL BLAINE**

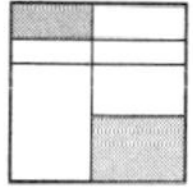

■ *I acknowledge the ever-present nearness of chaos and affirm that I can function in it and even sometimes tame it. When I love, I tame it; when I am creative, I tame it: so it appears that I possess at least a few solutions to the problem of chaos. But whether I manage to tame chaos or not, I will fearlessly allow it to inform me and my work.*

Character Flaws

"I was a very unpleasant young man. If I met the young Ingmar today I'd say, 'You're very talented and I'll try to help you, but I don't want anything else to do with you.' "

—**Ingmar Bergman**

"I have always been more interested in creating a character that contains something crippled. I think nearly all of us have some kind of defect."

—**Tennessee Williams**

"No doubt Jack the Ripper excused himself on the grounds that it was human nature."

—**A. A. Milne**

"Everyone is a moon and has a dark side which he never shows to anybody."

—**Mark Twain**

All of us do a better job of pointing a finger than of admitting our faults. Let us mind this truth and demand of ourselves that we act more humanely. Our defects are not just little dents in the paint; they are large screws loose in the engine. Unless we repair ourselves we fail ourselves and doom those who would try to love us. The artist, whose goals are large ones—to preserve culture, to work mightily, to transform matter—must reckon with his own character flaws, which do not disappear just because he has been called to be an artist.

■ *I will not excuse away my flaws. Instead I will better myself, for my own sake, for the sake of others, and for the sake of my art. I do not cling to the idea that it is fine to be cruel, selfish, and haughty, just because I am an artist: I reject that idea. I would just as soon be known for my character as for my songs or sculptures.*

Choices

An inability to choose is a hallmark of anxiety. But an ability to choose is a necessity for the artist. To decide to reach for this blue and not that one, to switch styles or subject matter, to move, in the middle of a sentence, in one direction or another, to commit to this book when that one is also calling, are the sorts of choices that artists *must* make if they are to function. The too-anxious artist, afraid to choose, will halt dead in the water. Self-love and the demands of authentic living require that she embrace that anxiety and get on with the business of selecting and deciding.

"Some rainy winter Sunday when there's a little boredom, you should carry a gun. Not to shoot yourself, but to know exactly that you're always making a choice."

—**Lina Wertmuller**

"All painting is an accident. But it's also not an accident, because one must select what part of the accident one chooses to preserve."

—**Francis Bacon**

"How do you paint yellow wheat against a yellow sky? You paint it jet black."

—**Ben Shahn**

"We are as much informed of a writer's genius by what he selects as by what he originates."

—**Ralph Waldo Emerson**

■ *I can choose and I must choose. Many times I've felt as if I couldn't; many times I've found myself weakened by doubt and anxiety. But I will do better: I will trust myself more, trust that I will survive my mistakes, trust that I am an artist. I will learn to choose effortlessly and effectively, without a lot of pain and wasted motion.*

Commitment

"I had trouble making a commitment to songwriting until I was thirty-two, even after I'd won fifteen or twenty BMI awards."

—**Gerry Goffin**

"I had gotten to the point where I was either going to play the violin much better or I was going to break it over my knee."

—**Ellen Taaffe Zwilich**

"The only true happiness comes from squandering ourselves for a purpose."

—**John Mason Brown**

"Example moves the world more than doctrine."

—**Henry Miller**

Is commitment more about duty or love? Is it something one demands of oneself or does it flow naturally, given the right circumstances? Committing to one symphony may mean exactly that one is in love with the main theme and wants to pursue it. But committing to the next may mean that one has accepted a fine commission and now must work diligently. It can be duty; it can be love; it can flow naturally; it can be a hard-fought act of will. But regardless of how it arises, commitment is the goal: a pledge to the work rooted in the deepest authority of self.

■ *I will become expert at commitment for the sake of those times when I must commit out of duty, and not love—on days when I hate the work, on nights when I wish the studio would burn down. To commit when I feel inspired, capable, and grand is one thing; I will also commit on days when I feel dull, blue, and insignificant.*

COMMUNITY

Artists are full of community feeling but, caught in the snare of this time and place, struggling to eke out a living, divided by rivalries, envy, and limited opportunities, and obsessed with maintaining their independence, they rarely manage to find rich ways of coming together. But exceptions arise: the alive collective, the intimate band, the truly supportive support group. Let each of us dream of a community of artists and work to make that dream a reality.

"Science has made the world a neighborhood, but it will take love to make it a sisterhood, a brotherhood, a community of peace with justice."

—ELIZABETH M. SCOTT

"Absolute individualism is an absurdity."

—HENRI-FRÉDÉRIC AMIEL

"All of us who write work out of a conviction that we are participating in some sort of communal activity."

—JOYCE CAROL OATES

"I'm attempting to blueprint for myself the merger of two camps: the political and the spiritual."

—TONI CADE BAMBARA

■ *I affirm my desire to create community with my fellow artists. I want the intimacy of that community; I want to feel our shared power as members of a much larger body—a union of millions of creative souls. Who knows what might yet be possible in the way of artists' communities, if only I make my own sincere effort.*

Completion

"Deep inside of every human being is this feeling that nothing is ever going to be complete, that the circle will never connect—and that itself is the secret to infinity."

—**Peter Townshend**

"It is difficult to stop in time because one gets carried away. But I have that strength; it is the only strength I have."

—**Claude Monet**

"We follow the line of a contour from its nervous system to the exaltation of the author."

—**Valerio Adami**

"The reward of a thing well done is to have done it."

—**Ralph Waldo Emerson**

Although nothing is ever complete, artists still must complete things. They must finish their documentary film, even if more interviews might be helpful, finish their tour, even if they are homesick. Some artists, secure in their understanding of endings, naturally complete things; but every artist, secure or insecure, must find the way to contain the sentence so that she can finally append the period. When a thing is not done, continuing to work is the strength; but when it is done, the strength lies in stopping.

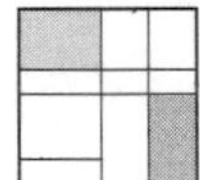

■ *Completing my work can give me real headaches. I have sometimes stopped short, before the work was done, and sometimes run over; I've sometimes revised too little and sometimes weakened the work by revising too much. But I will do better. I am an artist: I have it in me to become expert at completions.*

Composition

The connections among elements in a piece—in a dance, sculpture, play, or song—are found not according to the fineness of the outline the artist begins with but according to how well the parts marry as the living work grows and changes. If those parts marry out of conscious awareness, a composition arises whole and easily. But that marrying more likely occurs over time—over good times and hard times—as the artist makes and remakes, figures and refigures the jigsaw puzzle. A composition is an arrangement, built out of parts, that aims at seamlessness.

"The word *composition* moved me spiritually and I made it my aim in life to paint a *composition*. It affected me like a prayer and filled me with awe."

—**Wassily Kandinsky**

"All colors are the friends of their neighbors and the lovers of their opposites."

—**W. H. Auden**

"Composition can't really be taught, it is a lifelong learning."

—**Ellen Taaffe Zwilich**

"We move between two darknesses."

—**E. M. Forster**

■ *I love the act of composing; I love the things that I make, the compositions. Both process and product excite and delight me. I affirm my love affair with composition: I love that, even at this split second, out of conscious awareness new parts are getting acquainted and relating.*

COMPULSIONS

"I was so upset yesterday that I made the blunder of throwing myself in the water. Fortunately, there were no bad results."

—**CLAUDE MONET**

"Powerful men who have powerful passions use much of their strength in forging chains for themselves."

—**G. K. CHESTERTON**

"Cocaine isn't habit-forming. I should know—I've been using it for years."

—**TALLULAH BANKHEAD**

"Once I was beset by anxiety but I pushed the fear away by studying the sky, determining when the moon would come out and where the sun would appear in the morning."

—**LOUISE BOURGEOIS**

It is disappointing and a bad shock to the system for an artist to find herself plagued by behaviors she can't seem to control. Maintaining that she is free, she is confounded and proven a liar by her own powerful, destructive compulsions. She drinks heavily, ruins her voice with too much singing, dates hollow men, and binges and purges. Then, out of the throes of the compulsion, she wonders with amazement: what in God's name gave that compulsion its power? But in its throes she is a puppet unfaithful to her own profound purposes.

■ *Some believe that severe compulsions can be defeated by medication. Some believe that they are best disarmed in a twelve-step program. Some find they can heal and transform themselves through long-overdue self-love. I will find the answer that is right for me: I will not let my compulsions rob me of my life and artistry.*

Concentration

Artists must learn to concentrate and must allow real space and time for concentration. Who knows how many artists fail because the light that shines through them is defracted in a thousand directions and not concentrated in a single beam? Concentration involves a purposeful quieting of the mind and the body, a focusing of the artist's inner light, a decisiveness in the face of anxiety. The laser beam is the artist's logo; distractibility the artist's nemesis.

"One type of concentration is immediate and complete, as it was with Mozart. The other is plodding and only completed in stages, as with Beethoven. Thus genius works in different ways to achieve its ends."

—**Stephen Spender**

"I prepare myself very intensely. I am at the theater four hours before the performance. It allows for complete concentration and preparation."

—**Natalia Makarova**

"My nature is orderly and observant and scrupulous, and deeply introverted."

—**Joyce Carol Oates**

"Concentration is the secret of strength."

—**Ralph Waldo Emerson**

■ *I must concentrate. To do this I need solitude, self-discipline, and the willingness to entertain my own thoughts. I will better manage the distractions in my life and every day provide myself with the gift of concentration.*

Confidence

"It was important that I learn that what I wanted was no different from what other artists wanted: confidence that I could be my own censor, audience, and competition."

—**Beverly Pepper**

"When I'm staring at a blank piece of paper, total doubt comes. And then the confidence comes, the momentum, and suddenly I find myself in the creative act."

—**Bryan Hunt**

"Go on working, *freely and furiously,* and you will make progress."

—**Paul Gauguin**

"I don't know what the nature of the universe is, but I have a good ear."

—**Mary Gordon**

Even the well-nurtured child, when she steps out into the world and resides there awhile, is apt to have her confidence eroded. Her diet of rejection letters, missed roles, garage bands, or uninterested gallery owners hardly fortifies her. Soon she can create a list as long as her arm of the reasons she has to feel unconfident. Then she must burn that list, stretch to her full height, provide herself with new words of encouragement, and reaffirm that she is equal to any challenge.

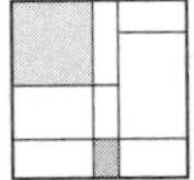

■ *I can't guarantee my own confidence, any more than I can guarantee my own courage. But I can grow ever more confident by working at my art, surviving my mistakes, achieving successes, and painstakingly investing in my craft. I need confidence and I will achieve confidence, for a lack of confidence ruins everything.*

CONGRATULATIONS

Ten canvases fail; the eleventh is a success. Does the painter congratulate herself? Not usually. After a long year the draft of her novel is done, the miserable and the excellent mixed together. Does the writer congratulate herself? Probably not. Rarely does an artist congratulate herself on staying the course; rarely does she exclaim, "That was impressive!" The part of the work that has not worked is much more on her mind. It is in an artist's real interest to congratulate herself more often: not out of narcissism, but in her role as her own dear friend and advocate.

"I feel that special secret current between the public and me. I can hold them with one little note in the air, and they will not breathe. That is a great, great moment."

—ARTHUR RUBINSTEIN

"I never believed in *trying* to do anything. Whatever I set out to do I found I had already accomplished."

—JOHANN WOLFGANG VON GOETHE

"One of my chief regrets during my years in the theater was that I couldn't sit in the audience and watch me."

—JOHN BARRYMORE

"There are some days when I think I'm going to die from an overdose of satisfaction."

—SALVADOR DALÍ

■ *There is no virtue in feeling as if I'm always failing. I have successes and I will honor them. I will congratulate myself when I paint every day for a week, even if no painting gets completed. I will congratulate myself when I create something that is flawed but alive and worthy. I will become my own cheering section.*

Convictions

"It is a blessed thing that in every age someone has had enough individuality and courage to stand by his own convictions."

—**Robert G. Ingersoll**

"The hallmark of courage in our age of conformity is the capacity to stand on one's own convictions."

—**Rollo May**

"I dip my pen in the blackest ink, because I am not afraid of falling into my inkpot."

—**Ralph Waldo Emerson**

"I paint not by sight but by faith."

—**Amos Ferguson**

The artist must possess at least as much conviction as does his enemy, the dogmatic, mealymouthed, anti-art bigot. The bigot has ugly, powerful convictions; and if the artist is not himself strong, if he too often questions his motives, products, and reasons for being, the bigot will suppress him, subvert him, and elbow him right off the face of the earth. A conviction in and of itself is no great thing, for any fool may have one; but humanitarian convictions are the linchpins of our salvation, and these an artist must champion.

■ *I will hold righteous convictions and act on them. This means that I will battle the dogmatic, the intolerant, the authoritarian, the great many enemies of art and freedom. When I falter and lose my determination, as I will, I will rise up again, strong and full of conviction.*

Courage

At birth, each of us gets a note slipped under our pillow: "Well, child, have you the courage? Have you the courage, child, to do what's right? The courage to be an artist? The courage to be human? Will the ten thousand things of the world wear you out, blind you, or break your heart? Can you stand the countless rejections, the thousand mistakes you must make as you paint or write poetry, the failed bands and short stories that deliver no epiphanies?" So the test begins; and it is never completed.

"No one understands the brutality of show business unless they do a musical that's in trouble out of town."

—Donna McKechnie

"When you try to do something you've never done before, you risk falling on your face."

—Ellen Taaffe Zwilich

"One thinks like a hero to behave like a merely decent human being."

—May Sarton

"The artist is the world's scapegoat."

—Jacob Epstein

■ *While I cannot do the just and fearless thing every single time, I will show more courage than I had ever thought possible. I will battle through blocks, fashion a career, and demonstrate my humanity. I have the courage of an artist.*

CRAFT

"That's success—to have crafted something that actors who are committed to *their* craft are interested in."

—KATHERINE LONG

"Painting is easy when you don't know how, but very difficult when you do."

—EDGAR DEGAS

"Those who write clearly have readers."

—ALBERT CAMUS

"Criticism comes easier than craftsmanship."

—ZEUXIS

Craft is honest labor. Craft is organization and clarification. Craft is the plumbing and leveling of material. Craft is the idea made real, one's ideals fixed for a while in reality. Craft is an answer to chaos and a substantial self-gift. Craft is the whirling body sure in its speed. Craft may be labor, but it is only drudgery to the person out of love with art. Isn't today a day to devote to craft? Isn't tomorrow? Isn't every day, routinely, until the end of time?

■ *There may be distinctions to be drawn between art and craft, but I am less interested in contrasting them than in honoring them equally. My work involves the mastery of craft and I affirm my willingness to center myself and the work, to be the good vessel and to make the vessel good. I am a lifelong student of my craft.*

Creativity

Mankind has long evidenced its ingenuity, but ingenuity is not the be-all and end-all of creativity. Every day another technological breakthrough occurs; but creativity is a rarer commodity than ingenuity. A creative person is the real sum of her parts: not a wily mechanic in a mechanistic universe but a glowing filament whose light illuminates a corner of the darkness. Creativity is the marriage humanity makes with eternity.

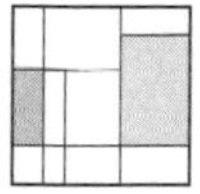

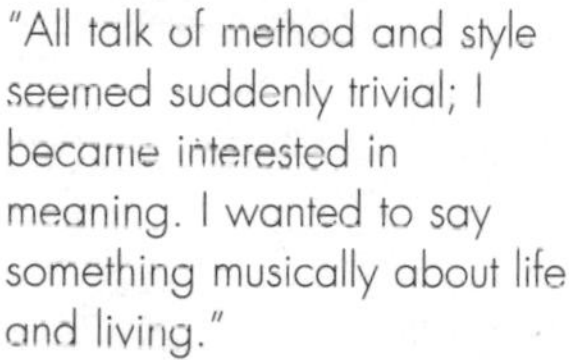

"All talk of method and style seemed suddenly trivial; I became interested in meaning. I wanted to say something musically about life and living."

—**Ellen Taaffe Zwilich**

"There is neither painting, nor sculpture, nor music, nor poetry. The only truth is creation."

—**Umberto Boccioni**

"The heart to conceive, the understanding to direct, and the hands to execute."

—**Junius**

"Helped are those who create anything at all, for they shall relive the thrill of their own conception."

—**Alice Walker**

■ *Creativity is a noble word, like justice, compassion, or humaneness. Creativity is a basic component of right living, for it is nothing less than a special loving attitude, a love of learning, a love of action, a love of self, a love of others. I affirm—simply, surely, unequivocally—that I am a creative person.*

Criticism

LISZT: "It is a march I have written on the death of Meyerbeer. How do you like it, Maestro?"
ROSSINI: "Would it not have been better if you had died, and Meyerbeer had written the music?"

"If someone says in print that this is the worst play ever written, it's hard not to lie down and weep, gnash your teeth, and eat a lot of chocolate."

—**Heather McDonald**

"Every actor in his heart believes everything bad that's printed about him."

—**Orson Welles**

"No statue has ever been put up to a critic."

—**Jean Sibelius**

Criticism will come. Fair and unfair criticism, useful and pointless criticism, sympathetic and mean criticism, the criticism that informs and the criticism that wounds. Should an artist attempt to duck all that criticism, the valuable as well as the vitriolic, and spare herself some pain? But that's quite impossible! For if she is seen at all, she is a critic's fair game. So hurray for criticism, if it means that an artist's voice is heard. Let the wise artist invite criticism and survive it when it comes.

■ *As an artist who shows work in the world, who bravely asks of an audience, "What do you think?", I am no stranger to criticism. I can neither prevent what a critic will say nor inoculate myself against criticism's sting. But I will find ways of living with it, sometimes learning from the criticism I receive and sometimes studiously ignoring it.*

CRUELTY

Artists at their best are not cruel and tyrannical, careless and indifferent. But artists are often not at their best. They are exactly human; like everyone they face the challenges of hating less, acting less selfishly, and making a better show of manifesting their humanity. Not every artist will be equal to meeting these challenges: we should not romantically suppose that an artist, by virtue of his calling and creativity, is automatically a good person. The artist, like anyone, chooses between cruelty and kindness.

"I know I was cruel to other children because I remember stuffing their nostrils with putty, and beating a little boy with stinging nettles."

—**VITA SACKVILLE-WEST**

"I am convinced that a person doesn't only love himself in others; he also hates himself in others."

—**GEORG LICHTENBERG**

"You can't eat your friends and have them too."

—**BUDD SCHULBERG**

"O, it is excellent to have a giant's strength, but it is tyrannous to use it like a giant."

—**WILLIAM SHAKESPEARE**

■ *I will not destroy others and I will not let others destroy me. If I am the target, I will protect myself or get up and leave. If I am the aggressor—the tyrant, the bully, the liar—I will stop right this moment. I am in enduring disagreement with those who would destroy others.*

CULTURE

"A nation in which a congressman can seriously ask, 'Do you think the artist is a special person?' is a nation living in cultural jeopardy."

—JAMES THURBER

"Culture is the sum of all the forms of art, love, and thought which have enabled man to be less enslaved."

—ANDRÉ MALRAUX

"Artists say: Stop, look, and *see* what is real. In our rushing world, no one has time for this."

—LANGDON GILKEY

"The dignity of a nation will not be judged by her ability to make money, but by her ability to produce art."

—WILLI SCHMIDT

When, as a child, the artist sat in a darkened theater, drank in a film, and began to be born as a filmmaker, he had no sense whatsoever of the cultural jeopardy surrounding him. But as an adult artist he inevitably begins to see the cultural playing field as it actually lies. This heartbreaking realization is not, however, the end of the story: the adamant artist grieves, regroups, and returns a wiser and even peskier defender of the principles of humanism.

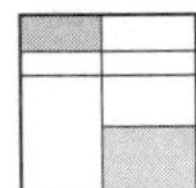

■ *Others may own the church, but I can be the mouse that runs across the organ keys and makes night music. I stand for art, culture, liberty, justice, humanity—knock me off my feet, if you like, but I* will *bounce back.*

Dance

The artist's bursting heart and burning brain have a body to play in, if only the artist remembers that she can just jump up and dance. But artists, too often trapped in their minds, are likely to remain earthbound. What prevents the painter from twirling like a dervish or the poet from leaping like a stag? Only forgetfulness: forgetfulness of how it felt to tumble, spin, dive, and soar as a child, when dance was natural.

"Dance is of all things the most concentrated expression of happiness and everyone needs to find happiness, to search for an ideal escape."

—**Violette Verdy**

"On with the dance! Let joy be unconfined."

—**George Gordon, Lord Byron**

"My best and happiest moments are on the stage. It is then I feel completely natural and am myself."

—**Natalia Makarova**

"All those mirrors keep pulling you back. You keep on seeing yourself—thousands of you."

—**Deanne Bergsma**

■ *I once was a dancer and I can be a dancer again. Is my studio only for painting? My den only for cogitating? My garage only for band practice? No! Every space is a space for dancing. I will not forget what motion means to my well-being; I will not forget how fine and human it is to dance.*

Day Jobs

"How to earn money while looking for work is a neat trick. The bottom line is to face this reality with dignity—something that provides a lifelong challenge for many of us."

—**Alan Thicke**

"It's unfortunate that an artist has to train in something else, in order to survive and pay the bills."

—**Susan Schwalb**

"How much time we lose in seeking our daily bread!"

—**Paul Gauguin**

"Music requires that a man give himself entirely to it, but the world does not wholly agree with this. It demands that he learn and attempt other things."

—**Georg Philipp Telemann**

How many day jobs will an artist work in a lifetime? Far too many. It is altogether absurd and unnecessary that she wait tables, learn the mechanics of spreadsheets, or spray perfume on passing customers. But these are things she will likely have to do. In this culture, there are precious few alternative answers. But at least she will gain a real experience of life from her day jobs; and she may even fashion a second career into which she can pour some love and meaning.

■ *I understand that I need money to live. I will approach the issue of money consciously, looking for solutions that free me from the forced labor of day jobs. But while I work my day job, I'll act honorably and bring my artist's eye and heart with me.*

Defenses

If a workable defensive structure is like a warm, protective overcoat, necessary in winter and reasonable even in the spring and fall, an unworkable defensive structure is like a year-round suit of armor. What is meant to protect us can just as easily suffocate us, so that we end up spending our time immobilized. The artist, who must venture into the studio and risk there, and then venture into the marketplace and risk again, is obliged to learn how her defenses work, so that she can drop and raise her guard instantly.

"Surrender of the artist to the world is almost always automatically bound up with an attitude of defense and protection, so that the artist never seems to belong completely."

—**Henry Lowenfeld**

"People ask for criticism but they only want praise."

—**W. Somerset Maugham**

"He who makes excuses accuses himself."

—**French proverb**

"A man can fail many times, but he isn't a failure until he begins to blame somebody else."

—**John Burroughs**

■ *I understand that some sort of protective covering is a necessity. But I will not so armor myself that I turn a blind eye to reality, act cruelly, or crawl into a cocoon. I will confidently risk encounters in the world with only a minimum of defensiveness.*

DENSITY

"Art is the incomprehensible density of cosmic forces compressed into a small space."

—**DAVID BOMBER**

"I have become aware of this: the earth breathes, smells, listens, and feels in all its little parts."

—**EGON SCHIELE**

"A good question is never answered."

—**JOHN CIARDI**

"I am governed by the pull of a sentence as the pull of a fabric is governed by gravity."

—**MARIANNE MOORE**

The more information we gather, the more we recognize that the world is not made up of facts and figures. Artists, interested in the density of matter and able to comprehend and communicate that density, may become as engrossed in and seduced by superficialities as the next person. But they have it in them to recover their balance and refocus on the mysteries that striate the universe and give it its density.

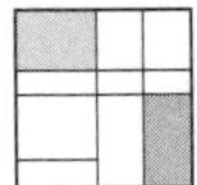

■ *Why should the simplest tune affect us so greatly? Why should mere patches of color cause great movements in the mind? Why should a sentence be able to capture and restrain chaos? I affirm my ties to the density, and not the nullity of the universe, a density caused by the participation of the unknowable with the perfectly plain and the ordinary.*

Depression

The artist's personality, built upon strong desires and compassionate vision, is by its nature prone to depression. Therefore an artist will be visited by depression as a matter of course; his job is to recognize how his own thoughts and feelings contribute to his sadness. He can discourage these visits by affirming his freedom and worth, by remembering to love, and by gently encouraging himself to believe in a world of renewed possibilities. Depression may be natural, but still the artist can dispute and overcome it.

"Every act of life, from the morning toothbrush to the friend at dinner, became an effort. I hated the night when I couldn't sleep and I hated the day because it went toward night."

—**F. Scott Fitzgerald**

"The pain is unrelenting; one does not abandon, even briefly, one's bed of nails, but is attached to it wherever one goes."

—**William Styron**

"No one ever lacks a good reason for suicide."

—**Cesare Pavese**

"A real depression can make a writer impotent."

—**Isaac Bashevis Singer**

■ *I understand that depression is likely to be part of my life. There are reasons for these visitations occurring; but I will dispute them and not get into the habit of encouraging them. I prefer not to be depressed: I will make a sincere effort to honor this preference.*

Depth

"Sometimes spectators of the Noh say, 'The moments of no action are the most enjoyable.' This is due to the underlying spiritual strength of the actor who unremittingly holds the attention of the audience."

—**Zeami Motokiyo**

"I, too, find the flower beautiful in its outward appearance: but a deeper beauty lies concealed within."

—**Piet Mondrian**

"Paint the essential character of things."

—**Camille Pissarro**

"The circle of the compass does not invite scrutiny. The circle of the full moon is full of incident."

—**Rex Cole**

Artists have it in them to feel depth in the universe, depth in other human beings, and depth in themselves. But the distracted, beleaguered artist can spend long stretches living shallowly and not deeply. Too much chitchat and passivity, too many irritations and dilemmas, too little love and affection, too little real work done or contemplated, and a smog of shallowness envelops the artist, making breathing difficult.

■ *I will live deeply. Skimming the surface of life is a human weakness I will not tolerate in myself: I will strive to overcome my fears, grow clearer-eyed, and bravely encounter that which is deepest in me and in everything around me.*

Desire

Artists have wild desires and a terrible hunger to achieve. They crave stardom, recognition, applause, praise, fat checks, astounding reviews, a splendid body of work, a breathtaking career. But all this desiring is a very mixed blessing. Without it they haven't the juice for striving or loving. But desire also can make them greedy and turn dreams into unrealizable obsessions. It is splendid that the artist wants, and may she continue to passionately want; but may she also moderate her desires and hungers.

"I don't want to discount talent and ability, but I still maintain that a lot of it is just sheer desire."

—**Don Henley**

"I am overrun, infested with a menagerie of desires."

—**Elizabeth Smart**

"I still have an insane drive to create and express myself, and it'll never stop because I don't know how to stop it."

—**Graham Nash**

"I want to be everybody, and I want to be everything. One life is not enough."

—**Vladimir Sokoloff**

■ *I am a creature with desires. I acknowledge the fire in me, the vitality: I know that it is real and valuable, but also dangerous. I affirm my own aspirations, but I will not become a hunger artist, unable to find food to like, forever starving and dissatisfied with my lot. I will desire, but I won't let desire destroy me.*

DESTINY

"There's a Chinese proverb that I think is true: You often find your destiny on the path you take to avoid it."

—**HECTOR ELIZONDO**

"It's so hard to retain what your purpose is—or to even realize what it is."

—**SINÉAD O'CONNOR**

"Man's destiny is nowhere spelled out, nor is his duty."

—**JACQUES MONOD**

"It is absurd to say that the age of miracles is past. It has not yet begun."

—**OSCAR WILDE**

The artist takes it upon herself to mold her destiny. This is the profound existential task confronting every artist, but it is a task that can only be attempted in the unaccommodating real world. The real world wounds her, deflects her, confuses her, deters her, and even obscures her path entirely. It is therefore an artist's job to reinvent herself regularly, brushing the cobwebs from her eyes so that she may again see where her destiny resides.

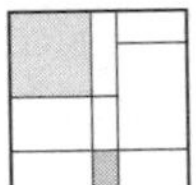

■ *I will act as if I have a singular destiny, one that involves my speaking in my own voice. It is a destiny that must be partly predetermined, so that its actual shape may not be the one I desire: I accept that lack of possibility but will redouble my efforts to create in reality the destiny I hope is mine.*

Directing

Art is manipulation, the management of material, the directing of fate into this short story or that, into this jazz band or that Latin fusion one, into this tall sculpture or that squat one. Who does that directing? The artist, whether or not she has ever directed an ensemble on Broadway or an orchestra at Lincoln Center. Among the spirited, productive artist's many identities is that of director: give her a script, $50 million, and a cast of thousands, and whether she is a painter, poet, or dancer she can leap to the occasion.

"A text cannot say everything. It can only go as far as all words can go. Beyond them begins another zone, a zone of mystery, of silence, which one calls the atmosphere."

—**Gaston Baty**

"A classic is like a hidden treasure. Its core is buried under so many layers of varnish that it can be reached only by patience and infiltration."

—**Jean-Louis Barrault**

"You must have the score in your head, not your head in the score."

—**Hans von Bülow**

"You have to work very hard to ground things like Siamese twins and kids with telekinesis in some kind of reality most people can understand."

—**Brian De Palma**

■ *I am equal to the task of directing and accept that one of my roles as an artist is that of director. I must direct my career, guide my material, and manage relationships in the marketplace. If I am not to drift, like a temperamental orchestra lacking a maestro's fine hand, I must provide my own guidance and direction.*

Disbelief

"It is not disbelief that is dangerous to our society; it is belief."

—**George Bernard Shaw**

"Every man prefers belief to the exercise of judgment."

—**Seneca**

"Believe nothing, O monk, merely because you have been told it."

—**Siddharta Gautama**

"Dogma does not mean the absence of thought but the end of thought."

—**G. K. Chesterton**

Artists disbelieve and dispute society's most cherished notions. This comes naturally to an artist; this is one of the jobs she was born to do. But what is left for her after the dust of the dogma she's exploded has settled? Not many footholds remain on the precarious ledge upon which she finds herself teetering. She must invent her entire philosophy and her reasons for being; and even these she may need to discard as her circumstances change. An artist may revel in disbelief: but it is an awfully tiring business.

■ *Championing disbelief is quite a miserable enterprise. I have to figure everything out for myself, then wonder if I've calculated correctly. I must have some beliefs, but at the same time be wary of believing them. Still, despite the absurdities and the difficulties, I affirm that to disbelieve is both valiant and necessary.*

Discipline

An artist may work all day at the office and then not get to his studio in the evening: is he lazy? He may jog five miles, but then not find the will to touch his novel: is he undisciplined? He may scrutinize every frame of his film, spending twenty hours a day consumed by it, and lose touch with his children: is he a lax wretch? Every human being is both disciplined and undisciplined: that is how we are built. An artist's fine goal is to manifest a well-nigh heroic self-discipline, carefully attending to all that concerns him.

"In order to be a good writer, you've got to be a bad boss. Self-discipline and stamina are the two major arms in a writer's arsenal."

—Leon Uris

"To enjoy freedom we have to control ourselves."

—Virginia Woolf

"Duty is what one expects from others—it is not what one does oneself."

—Oscar Wilde

"What I have set down in a moment of ardor I must then critically examine. Sometimes I must do myself violence before I can mercilessly erase things thought out with love."

—Peter Ilyich Tchaikovsky

■ *I can subtract indiscipline from my life and add more discipline. I know that however small the act may be—just a daily hour in the studio, just an extra hour of instrument practice—every effort I make toward greater self-discipline benefits me. I affirm that I can guide and control myself.*

Discovery

"What I discover while I'm painting is all-important to me."

—**Martha Clark**

"Composing is like driving down a foggy road toward a house. Slowly you see more details—the color of the slates and bricks, the shape of the windows."

—**Benjamin Britten**

"I cannot expect even my own art to provide all the answers—only to hope it keeps asking the right questions."

—**Grace Hartigan**

"Painting is a self-disciplined activity that you have to learn by yourself."

—**Romare Bearden**

It is shocking to realize how much there is to learn about oneself, one's art, and the world. The young artist knows everything; by thirty she knows significantly less; by forty she is brilliantly ignorant. If she is lucky, as she matures she grows as ignorant as a genius and is continuously shaken by what she manages to discover: by the earth shifting beneath her feet once again, by her own amazed, ringing laughter.

■ *I will join Alice and explore every rabbit hole, even at the risk of shrinking and expanding. I will join Huck and ride the river, even if con men are waiting. I will discover the essence of poetry, unravel the mystery of song, grasp the intricacies of color. I am one terrific explorer.*

Disintegration

Artists have it in them to disintegrate: the stressors of the world playing on the strings of their personality can cause ruinous music. Then come the Pernod, Jack Daniel's, heroin, ecstasy, visions of hell, self-hatred, ennui, madness, carelessness, broken bones, and daylong nightmares; the masochisms and sadisms; the despair and the living death. Can the disintegrating artist save himself? Since recoveries do occur, we can say: it is a possibility.

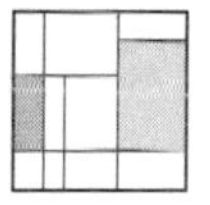

"Toward the end of my drinking career I was completely out of control and in a very grave place. I might drive a car, give a reading, set a broken leg, go to bed with someone, and not have any memory of it later."

—Raymond Carver

"Tangier doesn't make a man disintegrate, but it does attract people who are going to disintegrate anyway."

—Paul Bowles

"Nothing is true and everything is permitted."

—William S. Burroughs

"Agonies thrilled through me as if my blood were running ice cold in my veins. I stopped composing. My mind became feebler as my feelings grew more intense."

—Hector Berlioz

■ *I will dispute my own disintegration. If a hundred forces conspire to send me on a downward spiral, if I find myself living in collapse and ruin, I resolve to take a last heroic stand against annihilation. I am worth the effort it takes not to disintegrate.*

DOUBTS

"Doubts must be resolved alone within the soul. Otherwise one would profane one's own powerful solution."

—**WASSILY KANDINSKY**

"The first key to wisdom is assiduous and frequent questioning."

—**PETER ABELARD**

"Too much polishing weakens rather than improves a work."

—**PLINY THE YOUNGER**

"Doubt is what gets you an education."

—**WILSON MIZNER**

There are only two kinds of doubts, the ones to cherish, which arise from our openness, aliveness, curiosity, and risk-taking, and the ones to dispute, which arise from self-hatred and a lack of self-trust. Ah, but which are which? Do I doubt the painting I've just painted because it is not right or because I can never like what I do? Do I doubt my next documentary because it has a central flaw or because it frightens me? Yes, to be able to doubt is a blessing; but to despise oneself is a curse.

■ *I see that doubt has two faces, one the heroic face of the eternal questioner, the other the defeated face of the constant worrier. I affirm that I will doubt only when I sincerely doubt and not when I fearfully doubt. I will learn this difference, befriending right doubt and disputing the other.*

Dreams

There are innumerable ways that an artist dreams. She dreams at night, she daydreams, she dreams about what she wants, she dreams of nothing, and in that stillness songs and stories come. She dreams of other places, other times; she dreams up worlds; she sees in reality the dream, and in dreams reality. But indwelling is where terrors also live. It is the artist's job to dream but also to protect herself from monsters, to indwell but also to clean inner house. If too much misery and madness join her there, her valuable dreams will get run off by nightmares.

"It may be that those who do most, dream most."

—Stephen Leacock

"Looking at the stars always makes me dream."

—Vincent van Gogh

"The enquiry into a dream is another dream."

—George Savile, Marquis of Halifax

"Always dream and shoot higher than you know how to. Don't bother just to be better than your contemporaries or predecessors. Try to be better than yourself."

—William Faulkner

■ *I am a dreamer. I love to dream, I mean to dream, I will always dream. Dreaming is optimism, my imagination at play, life itself. When I stop dreaming the lights go out. I will take care of my indwelling and safeguard it against the terrible dreams that also arrive at a dreamer's doorstep.*

DYSFUNCTION

"Painting is no problem. The problem is what to do when you're not painting."

—**JACKSON POLLOCK**

"I was brought up in a clergyman's household, so I am a first-class liar."

—**SYBIL THORNDIKE**

"Our poisoned hearts must be cured."

—**ALBERT CAMUS**

"I am out of tune."

—**PINDAR**

"The nature of anguish is translated into different forms."

—**FRANZ KLINE**

Dysfunction is an odd, unbeautiful word used to describe mean-spirited relationships, self-unfriendliness, and poison accumulating in the human heart. What is not functioning? The better part of one's nature. An artist who can't help but involve herself with alcoholic lovers, who scratches her arms and destroys her canvases, who refuses help and ignores her responsibilities, has poison in her system. This unwellness runs deep, but can still be touched by self-love and self-awareness.

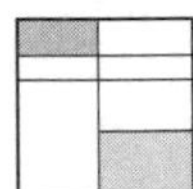

■ *The unwellness I experience is nothing I esteem or mean to cultivate. I have no vested interest in sadness and misery; I really do not want to harm myself or others. I suspect that the road back is a long and winding one, but I will fully participate in the healing I desire.*

Eccentricities

Artists have it in them both to be eccentric and to be ruined by their eccentricities. That an artist can lose himself in the middle of dinner because his mind has turned to dance is splendid; that he actually dances off between the main course and dessert may signal that his mind is cracking. Can an artist support his own eccentric qualities while avoiding bizarreness and madness? Can he assert his freedom without stretching his psychological resources to the limit? These are an artist's perennial challenges.

"People like eccentrics. Therefore they will leave me alone, saying that I am a 'mad clown.' "

—Vaslav Nijinsky

"People think I'm eccentric, cranky. If I'm eccentric because I've never been into mainstream things, then I am eccentric."

—Van Morrison

"Be virtuous and you will be eccentric."

—Mark Twain

"I have a lot of tics and phobias. I hate to travel. I hate to go to festivals. I hate it when somebody gets close behind me. I'm scared of the darkness. I hate open doors."

—Ingmar Bergman

■ *What others mean by eccentricity is to me simply the manifestation of my alive, idiosyncratic, individual nature. Therefore I will be eccentric. But I must carefully monitor my peculiarities, for they can be signposts not only of my uniqueness but also of an incipient madness.*

ECONOMICS

"The superior man understands what is right; the inferior man understands what will sell."

—**CONFUCIUS**

"Religion and art spring from the same root and are close kin. Economics and art are strangers."

—**WILLA CATHER**

"Money costs too much."

—**ROSS MACDONALD**

"If you can't describe a book in one or two pithy sentences that would make my mother want to read it, then of course you can't sell it."

—**MICHAEL KORDA**

No one can avoid the realities of the economic sphere. A cleric supported by his flock is enmeshed in economics, an artist supported by his mate is enmeshed in economics, a student away at college is enmeshed in economics. No one can avoid this entanglement, for economics means nothing more than somehow getting what you need. The artist, as little as she may need, is as trapped in the dust net of economic reality as the next person.

■ *I will look squarely and mindfully at the economic universe in which I am embedded. I do not expect art to pay, but still I must live: how can I best accomplish that? I will not live for money, but I cannot live without money: I will confront this human-sized tragedy with as much grace and consciousness as I can muster.*

Embarrassment

The artist is a god, but he is also an idiot. That is the human way. He follows a fine book with a stupid one, a brilliant album with a dreary one, a smart career move with an embarrassingly dopey one. Many astounding embarrassments accompany the artist on his path. While they may make him blush, stammer, and run for cover, they must nevertheless be accepted and overcome. After the blush fades away, or even while he's still rosy, the artist must bravely and nakedly come forward again.

"The truth is that I don't like rehearsals. I get embarrassed hearing my own work. I assume that the cast is embarrassed to sing the stuff."

—**Stephen Sondheim**

"He sheltered from the rain under the drainpipe."

—**Persian proverb**

"I have the feeling that I've seen everything, but failed to notice the elephants."

—**Anton Chekhov**

"I've spent my life making blunders."

—**Pierre-Auguste Renoir**

■ *I mean to be seen; so when I stumble, my stumble, too, will be seen by the audience. I recognize that if I'm to be an artist I must sometimes look like an idiot and feel mortified; but I will recover each time and laugh off the embarrassment.*

Emotions

"When I am alone with my notes, my heart pounds and the tears stream from my eyes, and my emotion and my joys are too much to bear."

—**Giuseppe Verdi**

"If you're involved in any way with the theater, you'll be riding a seemingly never-ending roller coaster of emotions."

—**Maureen Pratt**

"The knowledge of the means of expressing our emotions is only acquired through very long experience."

—**Paul Cézanne**

"How much has to be explored and discarded before reaching the naked flesh of feeling."

—**Claude Débussy**

We are built to have feelings but also to be wary of our feelings. We worry that sentiment and sentimentality are too closely related. We believe that reason is a better guide than feeling and that emotions are even an archaic stumbling block to effective living. But a hostility toward feeling is its own sad tyranny. Mind matters, but our emotions and feelings remain signal realities full of truth and vivacity. The artist can't paint, sing, or dance without emotion: if he does, he is a machine masquerading as a person.

■ *I will feel, even if feeling feels dangerous. I will feel, even if I'm used to feelings feeling painful. I will allow emotion into my work, so that the work may sing; I will encourage it in my life, even if sometimes I am forced to laugh or cry out loud.*

ENCHANTMENT

Enchantment is the great truth and the great deceiver. The artist embraces enchantment but also reviles it, for what enchants may be the artful distillation of some good or some evil. The very idea of a life in the arts, of creating and performing, is an enchantment, and must be held like any other: lovingly, for nothing matters more, and skeptically, in case the mind has been misled, the heart deceived. Every enchantment, the artist realizes, is both a joy and a danger.

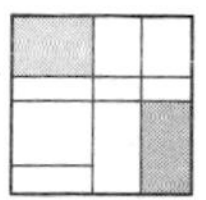

"Where is your Self to be found? Always in the deepest enchantment that you have experienced."

—**HUGO VON HOFMANNSTHAL**

"The state of enchantment is one of certainty. In the case of a false enchantment, our knowledge is self-deception."

—**W. H. AUDEN**

"It is the power of enchantment which matters."

—**RENÉ MAGRITTE**

"Everything that deceives may be said to enchant."

—**PLATO**

■ *I acknowledge my taste for enchantment, my eye for magic and wonder. I know that enchantment can mesmerize and seduce me, that I'm liable to see integrity in the merely beautiful, feel an epiphany when only some chords have been strongly struck. I will love enchantment, but not too blindly: I will close both eyes to listen to beautiful music while keeping a third eye open.*

ENERGY

"I had never seen such a great musician as that soloist. He looked very ordinary, but there was some inner fire in him that felt like a volcano."

—**RAVI SHANKAR**

"Art is the most frenzied orgy man is capable of."

—**JEAN DUBUFFET**

"I am not a human being, I am dynamite."

—**FRIEDRICH NIETZSCHE**

"I get up every morning with a desire to do some creative work. This desire is made of the same stuff as the sexual desire, the desire to make money, or any other desire."

—**ISAAC BASHEVIS SINGER**

The artist's inner fire may be so great that he can't contain himself, cool himself off, or live peacefully in the dull times between excitements. Or it may be so small, so tired a flame that he must drag himself about to live. Both the wild artist and the squelched artist have work to do on the thermostat of their being. Each must know his own flame; each must master fire.

■ *I aspire to high energy. I must be powerful and wild to catalyze the matters of my mind into art. But I must also be wise in taking my own temperature and learn how to cool down when the needle strikes red. I know that too much energy is dangerous; and that too little energy is tragic.*

ENVY

Envy poisons scientists, lawyers, shopkeepers . . . and artists especially. In the arts the gulf between the haves and have-nots is tremendously, even absurdly, large. Nor can time alone heal the wounds that envy causes, for the wounds remain implacably open. New books climb best-seller lists, new painters garner shows, new comedians gain stardom in situation comedies, new players become principals and concert masters. An artist must struggle to accept the shape of this universe—and achieve some important successes of her own.

"In place of an intensive cooperation among artists, there is a battle for goods. Hatred, partisanship, cliques, jealousy, and intrigues are the natural consequences of an aimless, materialist art."

—**Wassily Kandinsky**

"Every actor has a natural animosity toward every other actor, present or absent, living or dead."

—**Louise Brooks**

"The worst part of success is to try finding someone who is happy for you."

—**Bette Midler**

"One's jealous because one cannot live without love."

—**Eugene Ionesco**

■ *I acknowledge my own envious nature. I will love myself so well that in that wash of love I can accept the little I have, even if it is painfully little, while remaining adamant about achieving more. Envy hurts me: I will take pride in my ability to loosen envy's grip.*

Esteem

"You've no idea what a poor opinion I have of myself—and how little I deserve it."

—W. S. Gilbert

"I got a simple rule about everybody. If you don't treat me right—shame on you!"

—Louis Armstrong

"Short as I am, I played the tallest queen in history. I thought tall, I felt tall—and I looked tall."

—Helen Hayes

"I conceived at least one great love in my life, of which I was always the object."

—Albert Camus

It is not so easy to consistently hold ourselves in high esteem. Every day we do some worthy things but some foolish things, too: and the foolish things are the ones we remember at day's end. We eat a healthy meal, low in fat and high in fiber, and top that off by avoiding the studio. We write the hard chapter, but succumb to anxiety and break our no-smoking pledge. Our self-esteem is forever taking a beating, and sometimes the bruises run deep. But esteem is not a slave to gravity: it can rise just as surely as it can fall.

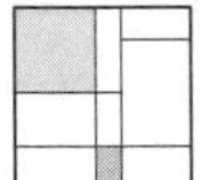

■ *To feel better about myself I must support my own best nature and live more wisely. To begin with, I will lavish a little kindness on myself; but I will also better become the person worth that lavishing. I know that my self-esteem is mine for the raising.*

The artist is in the moral minority. She knows that she has it in her to lie, but that she is not a liar; that on certain days she has it in her heart to eradicate the world, but that more often she would rather love it and transform it. She knows that sometimes the right thing to do is simple to fathom and that sometimes there is no clearly right thing to do. She knows ethics backward and forward: except, that is, when she forgets.

"It is ridiculous to say that art has nothing to do with morality. What is true is that the artist's business is not that of the policeman."

—**GEORGE BERNARD SHAW**

"I've handled color as a man should behave. You may conclude that I consider ethics and aesthetics as one."

—**JOSEF ALBERS**

"Always do right. This will gratify some people and astonish the rest."

—**MARK TWAIN**

"God is that inner presence which makes us admire the beautiful and consoles us for not sharing the happiness of the wicked."

—**EUGÈNE DELACROIX**

■ *I am an ethical creature. I don't always do what is right or always know what is right to do, but nevertheless I root in my heart for fairness and justice. If my art does not promote ethics, my art is wrong; if my actions are unethical, I am not happy.*

Excellence

"A tremendous amount of preparatory work and continuous training is necessary in order to turn your vague wish into professional excellence, so that in the end you are not a talented dilettante but a true actor."

—**Aleksandr Tairov**

"Very few people have excellence thrust upon them."

—**John Gardner**

"It's the best you can do that kills you."

—**Dorothy Parker**

"First I have tried to achieve the highest quality of technical facility possible so that I have at my fingertips the availability to create anything I want. Then I paint."

—**Audrey Flack**

It is not in human nature, and therefore not in an artist's nature, either, to strive for excellence all or even much of the time. More often we are slothful, careless, and only half-minded about things. Excellence means sweating, paying attention, correcting mistakes, gaining skills, not sleeping in, and not turning one's life over to treats and temptations. For the artist, it especially means staying the course, seriously and joyfully, and telling the truth despite one's own fearful nature. Who is equal to this?

■ *Excellence matters and I will embody excellence in my life and in my work. To do this I will wake up and work harder, fear and doubt less, and better focus on what is rich and important. Excellence can't happen accidentally: I must be instrumental in the making of my own excellence.*

Experience

We have enough experiences in a day to make art for a decade. But our distractibility, nervousness, and busyness, our lack of focus and our forgetfulness that we are artists, work to distance us from our experiences or keep them out entirely. So we must ask ourselves and even beg ourselves to let in our own experiences. The artist wants and works toward two things—to have experiences, and to really *have* them—and a third thing, too, of course: to survive them.

"Only when I experience do I compose—only when I compose do I experience."

—Gustav Mahler

"How vain it is to sit down to write when you have not stood up to live!"

—Henry David Thoreau

"The artist is a receptacle for emotions that come from all over the place: from the sky, from the earth, from a passing shape, from a spider's web."

—Pablo Picasso

"If an artist has no experience before he makes a painting or a sculpture, he is not an artist."

—Naum Gabo

■ *I crave life-enriching and art-enriching experiences. But I realize that I also defensively ward off experiences; and simply miss too many as life hurtles past. Where am I rushing? And why am I wearing so thick a suit of armor? I will slow down and open up to the experiences I want: I am equal to the patience and to the risk-taking required of me.*

Failure

"A good technician may lack passion. A passionate person may lack technique. Both may lack originality, judgment, or proportion. There are infinite ways to fail."

—Karen Laub-Novak

"I suppose I began to drink heavily after I realized that the things I wanted most in life for myself and my writing were simply not going to happen."

—Raymond Carver

"Failure makes people cruel and bitter."

—W. Somerset Maugham

"All men of goodwill have this in common—that our works put us to shame."

—Hermann Hesse

Artists know failure. It is not tragic that they know failure; it is only tragic if they know failure and little else, if failure is the flavor of their days. What will a thousand rejection slips do to a person? What will no praise whatsoever, no gallery shows, no record deals, no movie roles, no luck do? What doesn't kill the artist may make her stronger: but perpetual failure is in fact a killer. Success is a lifesaver; to achieve it, an artist may have to redefine artfully what will count as successes.

■ *I know I must live with failure—with far too many failures. Despite these failures, I will survive and endure. I'll work to counteract a buildup of bitterness and despair; and I* will *have successes, successes which I maintain are right around the corner.*

Fame

What sort of hunt is the hunt for fame? Is it a hunt for notoriety? A strange journey to become an icon, and not a human being? A voyage after astounding commercial success, one that must be measured in the millions of dollars to matter at all? Is it getting to be known by everybody and nobody? Is it something so odd and base that when you achieve it, you must then sneer at it and even flee from it? Might not an artist live famously this side of fame?

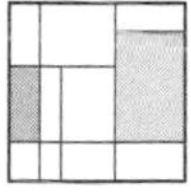

"I do not think about whether I am powerful. I do not think about whether I'm influencing people. I do not consider myself a hero or larger than life. Those are all mistakes."

—**David Crosby**

"Raising marble is evidence that a number of men have reached the point where the one they would now honor formerly stood alone."

—**Wassili Kandinsky**

"The real trap of fame is its irresistibility."

—**Ingrid Bengis**

"I like being well known. The recognition is important; it gives me a sense of security."

—**Marisol**

■ *The dream of achieving fame occupies a large part of my psyche. I will make sense of this disorienting and even dreadful desire; I surely want successes, recognition, an audience, and more, but perhaps fame is not precisely what I'm after. But if it is, then let me achieve it, for I will wear it honorably and well.*

FAMILY

"The family you come from isn't as important as the family you're going to have."

—RING LARDNER

"Father's birthday. He would have been ninety-six; but mercifully was not. His life would have utterly ended mine."

—VIRGINIA WOOLF

"I am in my studio all day working, often in that deep and violent way, and when evening comes and family life reclaims me, then I feel stabilized."

—LOUISE BOURGEOIS

"No matter how many communes anybody invents, the family always creeps back."

—MARGARET MEAD

The average person expects to raise a family. The artist is much less certain. She is built at least as much for the solitary, single life as for the suburban life, as much for her calling in art as for her calling in nature. The family in which the artist was raised will always have its effect on her, and with those ghosts she will have to wrestle. But the matter of the family she may or may not want to create for herself is vitally important in its own right, and worth her wholehearted consideration.

■ *I have it in me to go it alone or to participate in family life. Which will it be? Can it somehow be both? And if that happens to be the ideal, how can I achieve it? I will think through the matter of family as fearlessly as I can, employing both reason and an open heart.*

Fascination

Even an artist, with her billions of brain cells firing and her heart beating passionately inside of her, must actively caress wonder: for fascination, like the desire to play, can be eradicated by the rigors of living. Is the artist as fascinated at thirty-five as she was at seven? If she is, she has gone a long way toward inoculating herself against depression, boredom, and the power of distractions. Isn't fascination another face of the love an artist wishes to experience and manifest?

"He consumed a whole night looking at his great toe, about which he saw Tartars, Turks, and Romans fighting."

—Ben Jonson

"The spectacle of the sky overwhelms me. I'm overwhelmed when I see, in an immense sky, the crescent of the moon, or the sun."

—Joan Miró

"I would like not to reproduce but to reinvent the structure of light in a way pertinent to painting rather than to optics."

—Piero Dorazio

"Fascination is a key to productivity; it unites experiences; it is even its own reward."

—Erving Polster

■ *When I was a child, everything fascinated me. Water running in the street, a green centipede on a fallen leaf, the sharpness of a blade of grass: these things had the power to mesmerize me. Now my themes are different, but still I will live on the edge of my seat: fascination vitally matters.*

FEAR

"For many years we have suckled on fear and fear alone, and there is no good product of fear."

—JOHN STEINBECK

"It is what we fear that happens to us."

—OSCAR WILDE

"Very shortly after I stopped drinking and taking drugs, I realized that I wasn't frightened of the dark and that I wasn't an insomniac."

—RINGO STARR

"Fear percolates through all of a person's thinking, damages his personality, and makes him landlord to a ghost."

—LLOYD DOUGLAS

There are realistic fears that confront an artist—that a given song may be dull, that a given ceramic sculpture may go unsold—and then there are those fears—about oneself as a failure, impostor, and walking reproach—that seethe up from some subterranean place and jeopardize an artist's life and work. Reality an artist must embrace; but ghoulish self-disparagement must be disputed mightily. Do not fear that you are a worthless impostor: fear only that by such talk you are destroying your chance of being an artist.

■ *Why should I fear that I am not equal to making great art? What can the value be in scaring and devaluing myself? If I try, if I learn my craft and pour myself into something I love, what sort of mistake can that be? Will I have done anything but live my life honorably? I renounce those fears that arise from my belittling myself.*

Feeling

What do artists at their best communicate? If we had to choose between feelings and ideas, we might be wise to choose the former. Not the idea of injustice, but the horror of it; not the idea of love, but the warmth of it; not the idea of grief, but the pain of it. The artist, clever and quick-witted, may suppose that ideas are his chief currency; but unless he is also attuned to feelings, in life and in art, he will not move his fellow human beings.

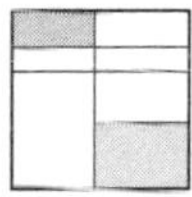

"I want feelings to be expressed, to be open, to be natural, not to be looked on as strange. It's not weird if you feel deeply."

—**May Sarton**

"I haven't understood a bar of music in my life, but I have felt it."

—**Igor Stravinsky**

"It seems simple to me, but for some people I guess feeling takes courage."

—**Aretha Franklin**

"Works of art are made of concept, material . . . and feeling."

—**Kenneth Martin**

■ *I do not always open up my art to my own heartfelt emotions. My feelings too often disturb, disorient, and even frighten me; but to deny my art the gift of my feelings is to make false, restricted art. I will risk real emotions in life—and risk them in the studio, also.*

Filmmaking

"If you can entertain them for two hours and have them talk about the picture for fifteen minutes after they leave, I'm satisfied."

—**Billy Wilder**

"Seeing a movie is a very solitary pleasure and permits people to indulge in something that is almost a vice."

—**Louis Malle**

"I sometimes go for the strongest, most vivid color on the palette, which in the case of movies is violence."

—**Brian De Palma**

"I'm not videotaping my life, but in a way I am trying to put certain things about myself on canvas."

—**Martin Scorsese**

We were each of us suckled on films. Has any medium more power to entrance and entice than that one? Can anyone forget the flickering images lighting the darkness that infiltrated our childhood? Film is music; film is the word; film is image; film is the actor; film is the director. Film is the editor's breathing and the cinematographer's eye, the costumer's memory and the sound engineer's inner ear. Any artist may look to film to be reminded about magic.

■ *I will infuse my art with the mystery of film. Aren't my dreams already exquisitely cut movies? Can't I bring the timing of film to my comedy routine? The marriage of music and image to my opera? The ultra-close-up to my sculpture? I've experienced so many films that I possess an entire second language: I am a multilingual artist.*

Financial Dependency

Where the money comes from that sustains an artist is one question. But in what relationship the artist stands to his sources of income is its own enormous question. Will he meekly submit at his day job and unleash his simmering rage at home? Will he remain with his mate for too many years, just because she's gainfully employed? Will he accept a handsome grant, even though he despises the conditions of acceptance? Dependency is a devilish thing: unavoidable as a practical matter and vicious in its psychological effects.

"No degree of knowledge attainable by man is able to set him above the want of hourly assistance."

—**Samuel Johnson**

"I attribute my success to three factors that have nothing whatsoever to do with musical genius: (1) an iron constitution; (2) a fair share of fighting spirit; and (3), most important of all, a small but independent income."

—**Dame Ethel Mary Smyth**

"I sent Matthew to college to make a gentleman of him, and he has turned out to be nothing but a damned painter."

—**Matthew Harris Jouett's father**

"Who gives the bread lays down the law."

—**Spanish proverb**

■ *I know that I need money to live. But even in the face of my financial dependency I will maintain a sound balance, rejecting both subserviency and ungratefulness. I will neither lick nor bite the hand that feeds me: instead I'll strive to shake it with dignity.*

FLEXIBILITY

"Interest in the changing seasons is a much happier state of mind than being hopelessly in love with spring."

—**George Santayana**

"We're living in an age now where you do television and you do film and you do stage—you learn how to do it all."

—**Anne Jackson**

"The creative thinker is flexible and adaptable and prepared to rearrange his thinking."

—**A. J. Cropley**

"To die for an idea is to set a rather high price upon conjecture."

—**Anatole France**

Are we flexible enough to paint realistically after a lifetime of abstract painting? To sing pop songs after a lifetime of classical training? Even though we require flexibility to negotiate our changing circumstances, we are rather built to anxiously turn away from alternatives. An artist's stubborn single-mindedness allows her to master her medium and achieve excellent results: but if stubbornness and single-mindedness are virtues, so too are versatility and flexibility.

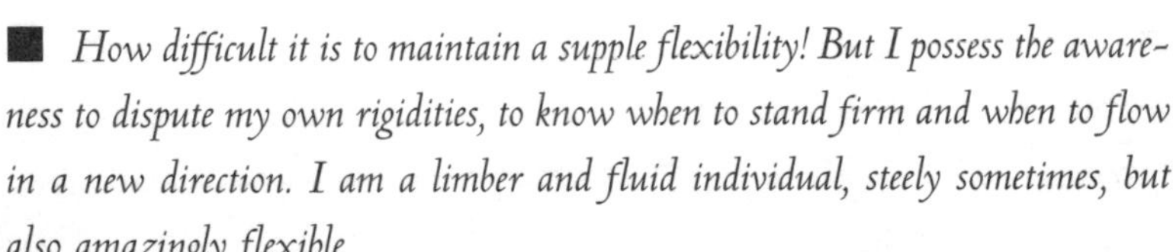

■ *How difficult it is to maintain a supple flexibility! But I possess the awareness to dispute my own rigidities, to know when to stand firm and when to flow in a new direction. I am a limber and fluid individual, steely sometimes, but also amazingly flexible.*

FREEDOM

Artists have a hatred of slavery and a love of freedom. But since they want to enter into book contracts, record deals, love matches, and other freedom-limiting arrangements, they must make sense of these passionate convictions in the context of human relationships. To champion freedom for herself and all humanity, an artist must dispute tyrants and act rebelliously; but to live related to others, she must make wise accommodations and good-spirited compromises.

"Heresy is only another word for freedom of thought."

—**GRAHAM GREENE**

"Freedom is nothing else but a chance to be better."

—**ALBERT CAMUS**

"This is the last of the human freedoms—to choose one's attitude in any given set of circumstances, to choose one's own way."

—**VIKTOR FRANKL**

"You are free and that is why you are lost."

—**FRANZ KAFKA**

■ *I will be free, risking the missteps that come with freedom. But I will not so exalt freedom that relating in life or in the marketplace becomes impossible. Freedom is a spectacular but not absolute ideal: I will wisely judge each situation and, when necessary, accept the limits put on my freedom.*

FRIENDSHIP

"There are about five people in my life to whom I really listen. They may not always be right, but they know what I'm trying to do."

—EMILY MANN

"One's friends are that part of the human race with which one can be human."

—GEORGE SANTAYANA

"I have lost friends, some by death, others by sheer inability to cross the street."

—VIRGINIA WOOLF

"I have no comrades—no one knows when I need comfort, encouragement, or a grip of the hand."

—FRIEDRICH NIETZSCHE

How valuable is friendship to the isolated, self-involved artist? Valuable beyond measure. Yet artists are often poignantly careless about making and keeping friends. A law unto themselves, they too easily reject or just forget about other human beings, losing in their understandable but wrong-headed maneuvers the support they crave for themselves and their artwork. The wise artist knows better: he makes friends and keeps them.

■ *However ambivalent I may be about relationships, I know that I am on the wrong path if I scorn friendships. I will be a friend and I will make friends and keep them. I will let my art bring them joy, as theirs will bring me joy: I am committed both to the idea and to the reality of friendship.*

FRUSTRATION

Every artist, however excellent his tolerance for frustration may be, must get badly frustrated in the course of doing his work and living in the world. The great novel he dreams of writing frustrates him in its execution. The marketplace then gets its licks in. Is the way to meet these inevitable frustrations to stop working? To despair and sleep long hours? To presume that others are having an easier time of it? Many artists can find no better solutions than these: but the determined artist brings artistry even to the matter of tolerating frustrations.

"Out of frustration, you do drugs when you can't write. On occasion that might work, but usually what happens is that once you've had one drink, you just want another drink."

—**STEVE JORDAN**

"I am very depressed and deeply disgusted with painting. It is really a continual torture."

—**CLAUDE MONET**

"Somebody's boring me . . . I think it's me."

—**DYLAN THOMAS**

"But worst of all are upsurging floods of hatred for the work itself."

—**DAME ETHEL MARY SMYTH**

■ *I can get terribly, painfully frustrated. But even as I feel the pain and disappointment, I will make a mental note: "I am not mortally wounded." Let me embrace the blue sky, hug my lover, put on music, and begin again: I will not quit on this, my only certain earthly visit.*

GEOGRAPHY

"I thought that by leaving Aix I should leave behind the boredom that pursues me. Actually I have done nothing but change my abode and the boredom has followed me."

—**PAUL CÉZANNE**

"I think perhaps there would be more anxiety in my work if I lived in New York."

—**EDWARD RUSCHA**

"All creative people should be forced to leave California for three months every year."

—**GLORIA SWANSON**

"You cannot hear the waterfall if you stand next to it. I paint my jungles in the desert."

—**MACEDONLO DE LA TORRE**

Should an artist live here or there? Since he must take his personality with him wherever he goes, he can't expect a geographic change to count for everything. But still there are real differences between a New Mexico town and London, between Los Angeles and the tip of Italy. Does an artist need the smells of Europe, the light of the desert, the electricity of the city, or the safety of the suburbs? Place does matter; the question of where to live and work is hardly an idle one.

■ *What place best supports me as a person and an artist? I mean to take this matter of geography seriously. I will become a master gardener, able to transplant myself from one soil to another whenever necessary; and if I can't uproot myself, I'll thrive right where I am, the hardiest of plants in even the harshest of environments.*

Gifts

Creativity is the gift that keeps on giving. As an artist nurtures her creativity, supporting it and fearlessly producing, she receives from herself ideas, images, guidance, and inspiration. These gifts she can expect, if only she will honor her own creative nature; if only she will pay attention to the knocking on the door, when gifts come calling. She can't demand that inspiration arrive at any given moment: she must simply do her work and get ready to receive it.

"You may work and work on a play and then another comes in the middle. You always have one play that comes as a gift, that's just waiting there and pops right up."

—John Guare

"One line came like a gift. It flowed out. I drew back and said 'thank you' to the room."

—Joni Mitchell

"It has happened more than once that a composition has come to me, ready made as it were, between the demands of other work."

—Amy Beach

"Every authentic work of art is a gift offered to the future."

—Albert Camus

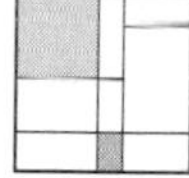

■ *How astounding that I can provide myself with precious gifts just by working! A melody for the final aria, a scene for the middle of the novel, and the sublime way to juxtapose scenes to start the film all come of their accord, just as long as I am an artist intent on creating.*

Good Causes

"We are all ready to be savage in some cause. The difference between a good man and a bad one is the choice of the cause."

—**William James**

"Imaginary good is boring. Real good is always new, marvelous, and intoxicating."

—**Simone Weil**

"If you stop to be kind, you must swerve often from your path."

—**Mary Webb**

"Good actions ennoble us, and we are the children of our own deeds."

—**Miguel de Cervantes**

Is art invariably its own good cause? And when it isn't, is it then something of an indulgence? Should all books expose corruption and abuse, or is there room for romances and potboilers? How are we to judge a documentary on sunspot activity after seeing one that details human misery? Can a musician play her guitar or a sculptor work her stone without worrying about her social responsibilities? All artists must question the role their art is playing in society, and consciously determine what that role will be.

■ *I love art and I love good causes. But must my art be an activist's art? Can I do whatever I like in the studio and then join a movement, or must my art itself participate on the level of ethics and politics? Whatever the answer, I will be sure to do good—not imaginary good, but real good.*

Gratitude

Can an artist appreciate the blue sky as the hundredth rejection letter arrives? Can she thank her lucky stars after another cattle-call audition has ended ingloriously? The artist shakes her head in the negative. But, doubtful that she has so much to be grateful for, she nevertheless feels gratitude well up within her. From what direction is it coming? Can she turn that way whenever she chooses? Is it possible that she can feel the joy of gratitude whenever she wants, just by inviting it to visit?

"There are moments on most days when I feel a deep and sincere gratitude, when I sit at the open window and there is a blue sky or moving clouds."

—**Käthe Kollwitz**

"I think my parents recognized something in me that they encouraged instead of deflated, and I'll always be grateful to them for that."

—**Graham Nash**

"Gratitude is the heart's memory."

—**French proverb**

"Gratitude is not only the greatest of virtues, but the parent of all the others."

—**Cicero**

■ *I am grateful to have been born one of the smart and conscious ones; I will show my gratitude in my art and in my relationships. I understand that a host of challenges come with being alive, but still I give thanks—for my passion, my ideals, and my truly wild nature.*

GROWTH

"Artistic growth is, more than anything else, a refining of the sense of truthfulness. The stupid believe that to be truthful is easy: only the great artist knows how difficult it is."

—**WILLA CATHER**

"I am progressing very slowly, for nature reveals herself to me in very complex forms; and the progress needed is incessant."

—**PAUL CÉZANNE**

"Everybody wants to be somebody; nobody wants to grow."

—**JOHANN WOLFGANG VON GOETHE**

"We teach people how to remember, we never teach them how to grow."

—**OSCAR WILDE**

Some artists grow, but many do not. As disturbed as Dostoevsky was, his novels climb and arrive at *The Brothers Karamazov*. But he is the exception; in America especially, much militates against growth and progress. The anti-art environment, the youth culture, the demand for sequels, the best-seller mentality, and a hundred other challenges assault artists and stunt their growth. The growth that an artist seeks is a fine combination of mastering craft, garnering an audience, maintaining one's mental health, and working mightily from an ever-expanding base of experience.

■ *I am determined to grow. I can't predict in what ways: I can't know the contours of tomorrow. But I can affirm my dedication to working at my art, studying my world, and securing loving relationships, especially with myself. I am committed to my growth: I will not cling to my comfort zone when it is time to venture outside it.*

HOLDING

Once an artist's mind is excited and a puzzle-shaped project is born, she must then hold on to it and carry it around with her, in and out of conscious awareness, as she works to create it. She holds it in such a way that it whispers to her while she works at her day job and makes dreams for her just before she awakens. If she doesn't hold her work this way, it will get swamped by everyday noise and vanish. But if she does, the project will form itself and grow, and soon she will find herself rushing to set down the alive thing she's been birthing.

INTERVIEWER: "Master, how did you think of the divine motif of your Ninth Symphony?"
ANTON BRUCKNER: "I sat down by a little brook, unpacked my Swiss cheese, and that darn tune popped into my head!"

"I have never solved a major mechanical or interpretive problem at the keyboard. I have always solved it in my mind."

—**JORGE BOLET**

"When I'm near the end of a book, I need to sleep in the same room with it."

—**JOAN DIDION**

"The defining function of the artist is to cherish consciousness."

—**MAX EASTMAN**

■ *My creative work must be held closely. I don't need to demand of myself that I think about it all the time; indeed, sometimes I must forget about it, to let it grow unobserved. But even as I forget about it I must love it and want it to live. My work is precious and infinitely light: I can carry it around with me wherever I go.*

Honesty

"Every time I paint a portrait I lose a friend."

—John Singer Sargent

"Character is much easier kept than recovered."

—Thomas Paine

"I accept reality and dare not question it."

—Walt Whitman

"Make yourself an honest man, and then you may be sure there is one less rascal in the world."

—Thomas Carlyle

"Craft must have clothes, but truth loves to go naked."

—Thomas Fuller

Honesty is a curious thing. Is it honest or dishonest to tell the truth about a friend in a work of fiction? To sing the songs that no longer reflect what you believe—the songs off your disco album or your religious revival album—but that your audience is fully expecting to hear? To endorse a fellow writer's book, even though you only half like it? Artists learn that both an amazing honesty and an amazing dishonesty reside within them, and that ethics is the exquisite sorting out of this human fact.

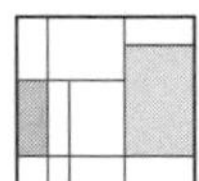

I can lie and I can tell the truth. I can be dishonest in such subtle ways that I hardly notice my devilishness, and I can be honest in such profound ways that sometimes I feel heroic. How human a combination! But even though I'm certain to go on telling lies, when it really counts I will succeed at truth-telling.

Humanism

What is humanism? The notion that flawed human beings nevertheless have it in them to build just institutions and societies, learn from their mistakes and the lessons of history, create things of value and beauty, and evolve in the direction of greater love, freedom, and tolerance. The objections to humanism—that it is unrealistic and utopian—do not sway the artist. She is clear that she is a humanist: for she sees something in human beings that moves and impresses her.

"The artist has a special task: that of reminding men of their humanity and the promise of their creativity."

—**Lewis Mumford**

"Don't people reveal how small their souls are when they weep and wail over Christ's death? Isn't the death of every ordinary person, in pain and misery, a much harder death?"

—**Emil Nolde**

"We are healthy only to the extent that our ideas are humane."

—**Kurt Vonnegut**

"Art is an effort to create, beside the real world, a more humane world."

—**André Maurois**

■ *I am a humanist. I believe in the human heart and in the value of ideals such as freedom and justice. I understand that this pits me against the mass of people, who prefer to live by one received dogma or another: but I am not daunted by large numbers. I am an artist and a humanist.*

Humanity

"My work has always been involved in exposure. The subject matter is the paint and the paint speaks of human needs."

—Joan Snyder

"I hope I shall be able to make some drawings in which there is something human."

—Vincent van Gogh

"The human image has never been forgotten in the arts."

—Germain Richier

"I would like, in my arbitrary way, to bring one nearer to the actual human being."

—Francis Bacon

Many subjects intrigue an artist. But isn't humanity an artist's primary subject matter? Isn't a painting less about formal balance and the dynamics of complementary colors and much more about one human heart sharing its secrets with another? A novel can be written in the third person, the first person, or even the second: but isn't its substance always the human spectacle? Isn't it the investigation of an artist's own humanity that really motivates and obsesses her?

■ *I take humanity as my subject matter. Whether I choose to make abstract paintings or earthwork sculptures, write shape poetry or pantoums, or play Baroque music or rhythm and blues, I am always addressing a single question: "What does it mean to be human?"*

Hushing

Artists aspire to a quiet mind, but like everyone else they are deluged by noise. Some of that noise comes from the furious cobbling going on in their inner workshop, where art is being built; but much of it arises from incessant worry and an attitude of self-reproach. To grow quiet is to love oneself better and let go of distractions; then the ideas and images forming out of conscious awareness can come forward to be caressed and examined.

"Most of the evils of life arise from man's being unable to sit still in a room."

—**Blaise Pascal**

"Men fear silence as they fear solitude, because both give them a glimpse of the terror of life's nothingness."

—**André Maurois**

"All the really good ideas I ever had came to me while I was milking a cow."

—**Grant Wood**

"No great work has ever been produced except after a long interval of still and musing meditation."

—**Walter Bagehot**

■ *I know the sort of silence I crave. To achieve that silence I will remind myself to hush: to actively empty my mind, to breathe away anxiety, to quiet all that unwanted din. Then, as I wash the dishes or prepare my palette, sit at the computer or take a walk, a great silence can envelop me, out of which my art will flow.*

I Am

"For years I had been haunted by the idea that I had no self. Or rather, that I had an endless supply of selves—an embarrassing state not experienced as prodigality but as absence."

—**Eleanor Antin**

"My playing is getting all behindhand, as is always the case when Robert is composing. I cannot find one little hour in the day for myself."

—**Clara Schumann**

"We change our opinions of ourselves so often. What the outside world thinks is only a small part of our image."

—**Carly Simon**

"That I exist is a perpetual surprise which is life."

—**Rabindranath Tagore**

I am an artist. I shape myself; I work at my craft; I live in the world; I make oboe reeds, mix blues and greens, cold-call agents, sing in front of a live audience. I exist and surprise others with my artifacts and my existence. I am an archaeologist, forever digging, and a reconstructive surgeon, forever repairing my cuts and bruises. I am one powerful self made up of so many selves that sometimes I throw myself a get-acquainted party. I am a human being and an artist: I really, simply, surely am.

■ *I am the person I create. I will make myself proud, mistake after mistake, rejection after rejection, foolishness after foolishness, by doing better and working harder. What finer way to build a strong self-image than by actually growing wiser and more capable? I am an artist creating an artist.*

IDEAS

The working artist is a thinking artist: if you take a peek at her brain you will see her neurons assiduously firing. She considers the landscape in front of her and determines to paint its bones, and not its flesh. She travels to South America and returns with musical ideas informed by the Andes. She edits her documentary one way, but in the middle of the night a new arrangement startles her awake. She thinks—and cherishes her thought processes.

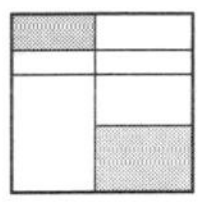

"All ideas are to some extent subversive."

—**Albert Gerard**

"Art is idea. It is not enough to draw, paint, and sculpt. An artist should be able to think."

—**Gurdon Woods**

"Because good theater appeals to the mind, interesting ideas are a prerequisite."

—**David Hwang**

"Take care of the sense and the sounds will take care of themselves."

—**Lewis Carroll**

■ *I relish ideas. I appreciate that it is dangerous to live too much in my mind and that my mental health requires that I quiet my seething brain sometimes. But I will not shy away from thinking: dumbness may be popular and pleasant, but that is not the route I am taking.*

Identity

"What is my identity? This question produces a kind of crisis in my thinking about my painting and myself."

—**Gunther Gerzso**

"I get asked to shows—women's shows, black shows—but I won't be bought until I'm asked to be in shows without race and gender adjectives in the title."

—**Maren Hassinger**

"If you're a composer, there's never a moment you're not working."

—**Ellen Taaffe Zwilich**

"Once a work is finished, I forget about being a composer and approach it as a pianist."

—**Vivian Fine**

Each identity the artist possesses makes its demands on him. If he is a Catholic, how will that affect him? If he is gay? A New Yorker? A southerner? An African-American? Should he strive to be a human being first and moderate his group feelings, or should he make important group concerns his own? Should he bring his many identities or a certain neutrality to the art he makes? And what will his identity as an artist entail? A whole lifetime will not be long enough to answer these essential questions.

■ *I am many things. I will not let one or another of my identities overwhelm me, for I am larger than and different from my various affiliations. I am not only a painter, even though I paint, and not only an American, even though I live and work here. I am affected by my group identifications, but first of all I am a member of the human race.*

Imagination

Does an artist need a surrealist's mind? Or is bizarre invention an overrated talent? What, to start with, is imagination exactly? Is it more about the dreaming up of novelties or more about pondering everyday realities? Is it more about inventing a lightbulb where none had been before or more about remembering the look of the sky at sunset? Each artist has this puzzle to unravel: what is imagination, and in what sense is it valuable?

"Let us proclaim that the sidewalk can climb up your table, that your head can cross the street, and that at the same time your household lamp can suspend between one house and another the immense spiderweb of its dusty rays."

—**Umberto Boccioni**

"The universe is real but you can't see it. You have to imagine it. Once you imagine it, you can be realistic about reproducing it."

—**Alexander Calder**

"The artist who uses the least of what is called imagination will be the greatest."

—**Pierre-Auguste Renoir**

"Imagination takes humility, love, and great courage."

—**Carson McCullers**

■ *I am not a machine spinning out fine fantasies: I am a human being on a righteous course. I will use my imagination not only in the service of novelty and beauty, but of truth and goodness, too. I can be clever and inventive, I can paint nightmare creatures or write the obscurest of poetry: but I value sincerity above cleverness.*

Imitation

"Out in the sun, some painters are lined up. The first is copying nature, the second is copying the first, the third is copying the second . . . You see the sequence."

—**Paul Gauguin**

"Some people think they have to take the same drugs as their favorite musician did. If they can't *play* like their idols, they can at least get the drug addiction right."

—**Robert Penn Warren**

"Do not think that it is possible to repeat another period."

—**Pierre-Auguste Renoir**

"The model is not to be copied, but to be realized."

—**Robert Henri**

Most people imitate. But while a novel answer to the question of how to make scrambled eggs or change a spark plug may be unnecessary, it is much nearer a vice to employ easy, formulaic solutions in the creation of one's art. Is this oak to be its own oak? Or will you glance at it but paint the oak you remember from an old master's painting? The wise artist recognizes when it is safe and perhaps even beneficial to imitate, and when imitation is a serious violation of what truthfully must be done.

■ *It would be outlandish and unproductive to have to put a personal spin on everything. Sometimes I will relax and imitate—while remaining conscious of my reasons for taking it easy. But in matters of real importance, and especially when my art is on the line, I will not fall back on imitation just for the ease of it.*

IMMENSITY

An artist may make a sketch of a thumbnail and feel the immensity of the whole universe inform her work. But if that sense of immensity should happen to elude her, if her work looks weak and puny in her eyes, she grows disappointed and frustrated. She knows the difference between the small and the large; and she knows that her job is to participate in and protect life's grandeur. So her guardianship of that immensity becomes a moral imperative: overwhelming, arduous, but integral to her sense of what it means to be fully human.

"A week ago it was the mountains I thought the most wonderful, and today it's the plains. I guess it's the feeling of bigness in both that carries me away."

—GEORGIA O'KEEFFE

"There are small fir cones all shriveled up, whose smell gives us such a feeling of immensity that one strolls through Fontainebleau just as if it were a dwarf's attic."

—NICOLAS DE STAEL

"Man is a fallen god who remembers the heavens."

—ALPHONSE DE LAMARTINE

"Modeling prevents shock. Without modeling depth is limitless: movement can stretch to infinity."

—JOAN MIRÓ

■ *I love the mightiness of life. The universe is immense and I am no less immense: if it produces exploding stars and kangaroos, cashew nuts and the human brain, I will produce my own equivalent astounding work. I will not shrivel up and waste my time on earth.*

Improvisation

"Improvisation is essential if the actor is to develop the spontaneity necessary to create in each performance 'the illusion of the first time.' "

—**Lee Strasberg**

"If you are playing jazz, you have to play what comes out at any given moment."

—**John Coltrane**

"More of me comes out when I improvise."

—**Edward Hopper**

"Improvisation is the expression of the accumulated yearnings, dreams, and wisdom of the soul."

—**Yehudi Menuhin**

When an artist gathers herself up, brings her training and her entire being to the moment, and holds at the same time a vast "don't know," art gets made. But if instead she discovers that she can't color outside the lines or begin a story until the plot is perfected, she is doomed to stall. An artist must risk making a mess and looking the fool: she must risk improvising. The wise artist knows that she must work on the spot, right where she finds herself, trusting her abilities and dropping her guard.

■ *I am not afraid to improvise. I won't put off calling an editor because I don't know beforehand everything both of us will say: I will simply prepare myself, dial the number, and improvise. I recognize that improvisation allows for encounters of the finest kind.*

INADEQUACY

Artists are quite aware of their own inadequacies. They know that they must reject the cozy lie that human beings are equal to every challenge, but that they are often inadequate still offends them. If this film is fine and that one flat, should an artist excoriate himself? Crucify himself if he can't write twelve excellent songs for his album, but only three or four? Hole up with a depression if his first draft is blemished? We are all inadequate sometimes: artists must survive that truth in order to get new work done.

"I think the only reason I ever used drugs was to overcome self-doubt. I didn't use drugs actually to create, but simply to buffer those feelings of inadequacy."

—DON HENLEY

"It seems to me that when I see nature I see it ready-made, completely written—but then, try to do it!"

—CLAUDE MONET

"I have offended God and mankind because my work didn't reach the quality it should have."

—LEONARDO DA VINCI

"In his private heart no man much respects himself."

—MARK TWAIN

■ *I am both talented and inadequate, magnificent and puny. I will work to the limit, honoring all that is great in me and accepting my sometimes tarnished human nature. I will recognize my own failures, forgive them, and then do better: I am an imperfect but still splendid creature.*

Individuality

"In art the search for a content which is collectively understandable is false; the content will always be individual."

—**Piet Mondrian**

"Certain defects are necessary for the existence of individuality."

—**Johann Wolfgang von Goethe**

"I'm against a homogenized society because I want the cream to rise."

—**Robert Frost**

"It is better to be hated for what you are than loved for what you are not."

—**André Gide**

The complete freedom an artist desires is simply not available to her. But her real individuality is no less worth protecting for that. She is not a domesticated animal, even if she must sit pleasantly in certain gatherings and make mooing sounds; she is not a tame conformist, even if she agrees to pay her bills and return her phone calls. Rather she is the maker of meaning, the guardian of culture, the conserver, the innovator, the stargazer. To be all that, she must zealously guard her individuality.

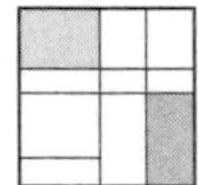

■ *I am an individual, one of nature's finest creations. I will think for myself and I will decide for myself. I will neither lose myself in others nor give myself away for the asking. I know what I prize and will continually honor: my individuality.*

Inner Child

Not everyone is comfortable with the concept of "inner child." Since a child can be cruel as well as joyous, dull as well as lively, it is not some surly self-centered inner child that an artist hopes to recover and nurture. It is instead such qualities as spontaneity, frankness, and a sense of wonder, qualities that the rigors of life are liable to inhibit. It is not the "inner child" that wants succoring, after all, but rather all that is finest in human nature.

"Every child is an artist. The problem is how to remain an artist once he grows up."

—**Pablo Picasso**

"You've got to keep the child alive; you can't create without it."

—**Joni Mitchell**

"No matter how old you get, if you can keep the desire to be creative, you're keeping the man-child alive."

—**John Cassavetes**

"My toy was my piano."

—**Alicia de Larrocha**

■ *I will play, smile, and stare transfixed at the rain. I will sing, laugh, and make up stories. I will draw, break my crayons, and not care that they are broken. I will walk on stone walls and dig in the dirt. I will not wrinkle up like a prune: I will be the ripe plum I am perfectly capable of becoming.*

INNER WORKSHOP

"Each actor has a little workshop inside himself that is his own. There is something important going on inside actors who really love their profession."

—**MARIA SCHELL**

"You feel like a prisoner if you don't create. You're jailed up inside of yourself."

—**EDIE BRICKELL**

"My eyes are gray-green, like the sea in Brittany, where I was born, and which is not a peaceful sea."

—**VIOLETTE VERDY**

"I had the landscape in my arms as I painted it. I had the landscape in my mind and shoulder and wrist."

—**HELEN FRANKENTHALER**

The artist is like a factory bursting with activity. Inside of him exists such a confusion of noise and energy, such a roar of ideas and bustle of imagery, so much poetry and music in the making, that he finds his brow furrowed as he tries to go about his business. But the brave artist accepts this inner tumult and lets the work of creating continue apace—even if to the world he appears oddly intense, and even if he himself would like a little more quiet.

■ *Since peace is not my goal, I will tolerate the racket going on inside of me; though it would be nice for my mind to take a holiday sometimes! Still, I will cherish my inner workshop, for real work gets done there. I'll oversee it without restraining it, and enjoy whatever pops off the assembly line.*

Insecurity

Late in life, shouldn't Renoir and Monet have finally felt secure as artists? But neither did. Shouldn't an artist, having toiled for years, having played a thousand concerts or sculpted an army of torsos, assume that he is equal to his next engagement? But, keenly aware of their limitations, artists often remain insecure even as their list of successes grows lengthy. It is sad that enduring insecurity should rob an artist of the joy he might feel, having put in a lifetime of honest effort.

"Fame, experience, and success do not necessarily mean that an actor knows what he is doing, or that he feels secure with his proven talent."

—**David Black**

"It's the way to get over a deep inferiority complex, being onstage; you become another person and shed your own frightened personality."

—**Shirley Booth**

"Being a celebrity made me so uncomfortable that I would have preferred standing behind the amplifiers."

—**Linda Ronstadt**

"I was—and still am—inarticulate in my real life."

—**Janice Rule**

■ *I am not equal to every challenge, but neither am I an impostor. I've had successes as well as failures: I may as well dwell on my strengths as my weaknesses. I choose to feel capable and secure: what can the value be in harping on my insecurities?*

INSPIRATION

"Writing a novel is like building a wall brick by brick; only amateurs believe in inspiration."

—**FRANK YERBY**

"You can't plan for a seizure of feeling, and for this reason I put everything else aside when I'm inspired."

—**MAY SARTON**

"I think people who are not artists often feel that artists are inspired. But if you work at your art you don't have time to be inspired. Out of the work comes the work."

—**JOHN CAGE**

"Inspiration is a farce that poets have invented to give themselves importance."

—**JEAN ANOUILH**

Inspiration is a reality. When the artist activates his being, awakens to his surroundings, and sets himself the task of creating, connections are made out of conscious awareness that return coalesced as inspiration. But no artist can wait on these bits, for they come unbidden; and if they arrive with fine regularity, it is only because the artist has been working. Working is the thing an artist must do, whether he is mired in the mud or elevated off the ground by a torrent of inspiration.

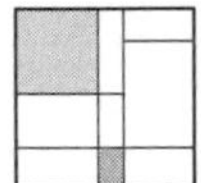

I believe in the inspiration I create for myself when I honor my artist's nature and diligently practice my craft. I will work whether I feel inspired or not: I know that if I labor with an open heart and an open mind, inspiration will come. I am ready to create it, receive it, and be swept away by it.

INTEGRITY

Integrity is a beautiful word. But trying to act with integrity is extraordinarily challenging. Why not accept a role in a movie with the potential to be seen by half the world's population? So what if it's really stupid? Why not accept the corporate art buyer at her word when she assures you that her company is righteous? Are you going to start a private investigation? How can it matter if the producer of your new album is cruel to the technicians? Is that really your business? Integrity is a beautiful word—and an awfully hard master.

"I am for integrity, if only because life is very short and truth is hard to come by."

—**Kermit Eby**

"The process of making art is about integrity and about defining one's place in society."

—**Catherine Wagner**

"I studied the classics and was filled with integrity."

—**Pam Greer**

"Integrity has no need of rules."

—**Albert Camus**

■ *I know I can disappoint myself sometimes and not act with integrity. To have the right principles and to stand by them, to work deeply and humanely, to stand up to bullies and tyrants: these are not such easy things! But I admire and aspire to integrity: anything less, and I am just not happy.*

INTELLIGENCE

"The intelligent man finds almost everything ridiculous, the sensible man hardly anything."
—**JOHANN WOLFGANG VON GOETHE**

"The visible world only becomes the real world by the operation of thought."
—**JEAN METZINGER**

"A man paints with his brains and not with his hands."
—**MICHELANGELO**

"An intelligent hell would be better than a stupid paradise."
—**VICTOR HUGO**

Can characters lead full lives without the guiding intelligence of their author? Is a concerto the product of a committee or of one mind in concert? Does abstraction happen of its own accord or must it be embraced as idea and reality by a shaping power? The answer in each case is the same: it is the solitary artist, through the operation of thought, who breathes art into existence. Artists think: they are an organ for ideas and a living intelligence.

■ *I know I can dumb myself down. Like everyone else, I can turn on the TV and disappear for hours. I can think about nothing or think poorly about what actually concerns me. I have, in short, the potential to squander my native intelligence. But this I would really rather not do. I will embrace, nurture, and encourage my own intelligence.*

INTIMACY

If an artist pursues solitude, lives in isolation, and adopts a fiercely independent course, he may not get very practiced at relating to other human beings. But he still possesses qualities—such as empathy, intelligence, and heart—that make him a likely candidate for intimacy, if only he valued intimacy more. An artist can sneer at relationships and pilot a solitary course if he must; or he can decide to love and embrace at least one other human being.

"The easiest kind of relationship for me is with ten thousand people. The hardest is with one."

—**Joan Baez**

"Love is the extremely difficult realization that someone other than oneself is real."

—**Iris Murdoch**

"I didn't think it was fair to pretend to give of myself when I was so selfishly consumed with my own drives."

—**Jackie Mason**

"I realized why my marriage didn't work out. For her to wait eighteen hours for me to take my mind off the band for five minutes was just not right."

—**Lars Ulrich**

■ *I desire intimacy. I wish to provide it and I wish to receive it. I want an intimate relationship with another human being, a relationship of love, friendship, sincerity, and respect. I may be a driven, solitary artist, but I want also to love and be loved.*

Introversion

"An actor may be shy, introverted—and the very fact that he's so sensitive may make him a better actor in the long run, after he's learned the tricks of the trade."

—**Edith Atwater**

"The man who has no inner life is a slave to his surroundings."

—**Henri-Frédéric Amiel**

"All the fame I look for in life is to have lived it quietly."

—**Michel Eyquem de Montaigne**

"I was never less alone than while by myself."

—**Edward Gibbon**

We have the sense that either one is introverted or one isn't; and that the introvert is bound to feel uncomfortable or even miserable in the world. But perhaps artists, who love solitude and likely consider themselves introverts, can hold a different position: that they may be introverted or extroverted, exactly as they please. Not only will this liberating flexibility help them in the marketplace, but it may release them a little from the joyless isolation they experience too often.

■ *I am an introvert. I love to work in solitude and keep my own counsel. But too introverted a life is dangerous: that way I miss the company of others, miss letting down my hair, miss all the silly games I might play. I can be either introverted or extroverted: the choice is mine.*

INTUITION

No muse shoots darts of insight into the unsuspecting artist. The artist, working with all of her senses and her whole being, takes in the world, analyzes it out of conscious awareness, and explodes with realizations. That is the whole of intuition; that is the secret of inner guidance. The wise artist opens to the world, trusting that her intuitions are just her well-made thoughts and her deepest feelings by another name.

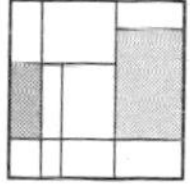

"I believe I rely heavily on intuition and depend on an intuitive response from my audience. I am a great believer in intuition, for men and women alike."

—**JANE FREILICHER**

"You have to trust your instincts. There's a moment when an actor has it, and he knows it."

—**CLINT EASTWOOD**

"An artist's flair is sometimes worth a scientist's brains."

—**ANTON CHEKHOV**

"The subliminal self is in no way inferior to the conscious self. It knows how to choose and to divine."

—**HENRI POINCARÉ**

■ *I mean to become more intuitive and more trusting of my intuitions. If an intuition has that certain feel to it, I want to value it and mark it well. I will rely on my gut instincts, for a world of my own wisdom is tied up in them.*

Jeopardy

"It seems I have learned to bear the anxiety of uncertainty. Now I accept that one can't know ahead of time what is on the other side. You might say my new works project a greater degree of jeopardy."

—**Anne Truit**

"Anyone who thinks places some portion of the world in jeopardy."

—**John Dewey**

"All great art is by its very essence in conflict with the society with which it coexists."

—**Erich Fromm**

"As soon as there is life there is danger."

—**Ralph Waldo Emerson**

To risk pursuing a career in the arts is to put oneself in jeopardy. Where is the safety in dance or poetry, the retirement benefits in ceramic art, the profit-sharing in Gregorian chants? And if, when you write your book, you remind the emperor that he is naked, the corporate sponsor that he is an ecological devil, and the cleric that he is full of cant, how secure will you feel? The artist risks anyway: he dedicates himself to a life of jeopardy.

■ *I would love more ease. I would love to be guaranteed success and a steady income. But my life in the arts will put me in jeopardy, not on easy street. I accept this destiny: I will find the strength and courage I need to stay the risky course I've chosen.*

Joy

Trapped in the dust net of the world, racked by consciousness, an artist experiences joy only rarely. She has no ambivalence about joy—she just loves it—but its unavailability disturbs and depresses her. Why is she joyous so little, when some part of her is so attuned to happiness? Have her struggles worn her out? To be sure, there can be no simply happy artist, for an artist knows and sees too much: but it is absurd and sad that artists get to experience joy so infrequently.

"The cyclone ends. The sun returns; the lofty coconut trees lift up their plumes again; man does likewise. The great anguish is over; joy has returned; the sea smiles like a child."

—**Paul Gauguin**

"I never achieved great fame—no heights of incredible glory. But I think that any strong endeavor that gives you a sense of joy is the greatest thing in life."

—**Sono Osato**

"Men without joy seem like corpses."

—**Käthe Kollwitz**

"Not joy is the mother of dissipation, but joylessness."

—**Friedrich Nietzsche**

■ *I will increase the joy in my life. I will let love rise in me; I will shout for joy! I will watch the sea smile, I will find happiness in the company of other human beings, I will open my window and let life pour in; I will sing for my own amusement. I will be joyous!*

Language

"I start from something considered dead and arrive at a world. And when I put a title on it, it becomes even more alive."

—**Joan Miró**

"All powerful language produces in us the idea of the void."

—**Antonin Artaud**

"Syllables govern the world."

—**John Selden**

"All the fun's in how you say a thing."

—**Robert Frost**

If an artist is inarticulate, it is only because she values language so much. Around her, people carelessly say anything: she holds her tongue. But that reluctance can leave her powerless as well as mute. Let an artist just say what she means in whatever language and medium she chooses: for there is value in what she has to say, in the humane truth she has to tell, whether or not she manages to tell that truth artfully. Let artists speak out on the issues of the day, or else glib tyrants will rule them.

■ *I love the language of my medium—the language of form and color, melody and timbre, the long shot and the tight close-up. I will make my language sing and I will sing the truth: I bear a custodial relationship to the language of art.*

LEARNING

If an artist stops learning, her creative muscles atrophy. But to learn everything about the billion bits of information available to her is an impossible, wrong-headed goal. Instead, she must guard that the inessential not swamp her while she minds that the essential not slip by her. To do this, she scans the universe with hovering attention, learning exactly what she needs to know and then beautifully transmitting that back to an audience.

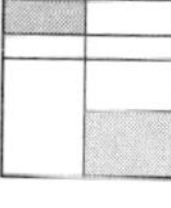

"My education was the liberty I had to read indiscriminately and all the time, with my eyes hanging out."

—**DYLAN THOMAS**

"Hearing my music on a regular basis became the best learning experience."

—**JOAN TOWER**

"Civilization is a race between education and catastrophe."

—**H. G. WELLS**

"To be an artist you must learn the laws of nature."

—**PIERRE-AUGUSTE RENOIR**

■ *I am an adamant student of life. I dispute my arrogant claim that I know everything already; I will do terrific battle with my defensive disinclination to learn. I affirm that in order to grow as a teacher, I must remain an alert learner.*

LIFE

"I would rather live at a heightened level than live the dull, commonplace life of the average person."

—**JANICE RULE**

"I need to feel the excitement of life stirring around me, and I will always need to feel that."

—**PIERRE-AUGUSTE RENOIR**

"May you live all the days of your life."

—**JONATHAN SWIFT**

"Art is an action against death. It is a denial of death."

—**JACQUES LIPCHITZ**

Artists embrace life. To embrace life means to make demands on life and to accept life's hard-edged tasks. It means paying one's dues, year in and year out, and reaping real rewards. It means experiencing life as an active and receptive instrument in a sometimes comprehensible, sometimes incomprehensible, always pulsating universe. The artist gratefully inhales life; she circulates it and exhales her own answering breath.

■ *I will stay awake and alive, even through my sorrows, even despite my failures and the failures of the world. I will not give up my right to live, not even for the soft, comforting sleep that conformity brings. Life is messy; but I vote for the mess of life, with all its unimpeachable reality.*

LIMITS

An artist who keeps his eye on the possible may achieve great, soul-satisfying things. He may enter into important relationships, write a worthy book, or spin across the stage. He may compose a song so beautiful that everyone, everywhere stops to listen. To do this no human limits need be transcended, which is lucky: because human limits can't be transcended. They can only be fully inhabited; the art of living is to fill a circumscribed space completely.

"Do we not find freedom along the guiding lines of discipline?"

—YEHUDI MENUHIN

"Art is limitation. The essence of every picture is the frame."

—G. K. CHESTERTON

"O my soul, do not aspire to immortal life, but exhaust the limits of the possible."

—PINDAR

"The deliberate expansion of means and methods does not automatically bring a new dimension of value."

—PIERRE ALECHINSKY

■ *I will not idealize life by hankering for transcendence. I will not lie and deny that life is limited. Rather I will embrace the limits that life provides and learn how to live splendidly within them, finding passion, love, and creativity there. I am a human being: I understand what that cannot mean but also what that can mean.*

LOVE

"Because there is a fear of sentimentality, love is not very often addressed—and it is really the one motivation in all of our lives."

—HELENE AYLON

"There is no love apart from the deeds of love; no potentiality of love but that which is manifested in loving."

—JEAN-PAUL SARTRE

"The only abnormality is the incapacity to love."

—ANAÏS NIN

"How, without love and the intuition that comes from love, can a human being place himself in the situation of another human being?"

—CARSON MCCULLERS

An artist sets herself many life projects, from truth-telling to creating, but all resolve themselves in the final analysis into various aspects of love. She doesn't paint to decorate walls with canvases: she paints because her heart is bursting. During the course of a lifetime of struggle, much interferes with her ability to love; but still she strives to love, for only when she is ardent does she live well. No other life motive is so worth an artist's time and effort.

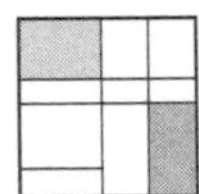

■ *I will love. I will engage in acts of love; I will become love in action. I may be doubtful that I can give or receive love or even that love exists; but I am not so doubtful that I will take sides against it. I affirm the centrality of love: the more love, the better.*

MADNESS

Madness is understandable to the artist. He does not understand its physiology or etiology: he simply understands that he has it in him. He does not long for it, for when it comes it is horrible; but he understands its secret lures and attractions. Wounded and tormented, he may finally venture in that direction: and if he arrives at madness, it will have a terribly familiar look to it.

"Not everyone is capable of madness; and of those lucky enough to be capable, not many have the courage for it."

—AUGUST STRINDBERG

"I have observed that poets on the verge of madness are often easier to translate into another tongue than are the sane ones."

—W. H. AUDEN

"I saw the best minds of my generation destroyed by madness."

—ALLEN GINSBERG

"Sanity is a cozy lie."

—SUSAN SONTAG

■ *While madness is a human thing, I do not welcome it. I will not invite visions or calmly accept my disintegration; if I can be helped by medications, I will embrace that possibility. Sanity may not be the perfect answer, but madness is surely a worse one.*

Mania

"She talked without stopping for two or three days. For about a day what she said was coherent; then gradually she became completely incoherent."

—**Leonard Woolf, on Virginia Woolf**

"I cannot coolly view anything that excites my feelings; and once that lurking devil is aroused, I lose all command of myself."

—**George Gordon, Lord Byron**

"I was overcome by an attack of pathological enthusiasm."

—**Robert Lowell**

"I am almost sick and giddy with the quantity of things in my head, all tempting and wanting to be worked out."

—**John Ruskin**

Mania is bottled anxiety, bottled excitement, part arousal, part madness, a vitality and an illness, an electricity that both illuminates and electrocutes. Everyday obsessive mania is the artist's lot, for when she loves her work and wants to birth it, when ideas flood her brain and she must arrange them, she is driven along by her own relentless passions. But some manias are twins to madness and must be treated as signs that the mind is breaking.

■ *I will gauge the quality of the manias I experience, living with and even encouraging those that are simply my vitality in action, but disputing, with professional help, those manias that are loud warnings that my mind is cracking.*

Marketplace

While artists fervently believe that the art marketplace was invented by the devil and remains in his henchman's hands, they have no choice but to carry long spoons and sup there. An artist's first step is to take a deep breath and really survey the marketplace: who are the players, what is wanted, and where is masterful work welcome? To communicate with others and to realize their own desires, artists must forge relationships in the marketplace, bravely negotiating the world of commerce.

"There is no mailing list of people who buy poetry chapbooks."

—**Mark Worden**

"Yankees and dollars have such an inextricable association that the words ought to rhyme."

—**Ralph Waldo Emerson**

"Literature is like any other trade, you will never sell anything unless you go to the right shop."

—**George Bernard Shaw**

"It is easy enough, once the commercial success of a book is an established fact, to work out a convincing reason for the public's enthusiasm."

—**Elizabeth Hardwick**

■ *I will act honorably as an artist, producing good work, even as I endeavor to sell my wares in the marketplace. I resolve to settle the inevitable conflicts that arise between art and commerce as consciously as I can. I will listen both to marketplace voices and to what my art demands.*

MASTERY

"Writing, like making love, is more fun when you know what you're doing."

—EILEEN JENSEN

"It's a wrong idea that a master is a finished person. Masters are very faulty; they haven't learned everything and they know it."

—ROBERT HENRI

"If Heaven had only granted me five more years, I could have become a real painter."

—KATSUSHIKA HOKUSAI

"Even in the works of the greatest master, the organic sequence can fail and then a skillful join must be made."

—PETER ILYICH TCHAIKOVSKY

Real mastery of one's medium and one's life is within an artist's grasp. All she need do is draw a thousand hours a week; play her instrument from morning till night; write page after page after page after page. To this simple work she must add all her brain power and her fiercest love. Then she must attend to the rest of her life, to her friends, her mental health, her environment, her world. That is all: in such a straightforward way is a master made.

■ *I mean to be a master at what I do. I revere mastery and accept that setting high standards for myself opens me up to anxiety and disappointment. But I embrace these risks: I will meet the challenges that stand between me and mastery.*

Meaning Sparks

Meaning sparks are those private excitements caused by consciousness and the world colliding. A glimpse of a patch of blue, a word half-heard, the look of a family straggling onto a bus, a chance conversation with a stranger—anything can spark meaning. And when those sparks fly, creative work begins to be born. Who hasn't felt those sudden shocks and illuminations? But artists do more than feel them: they savor them and use them.

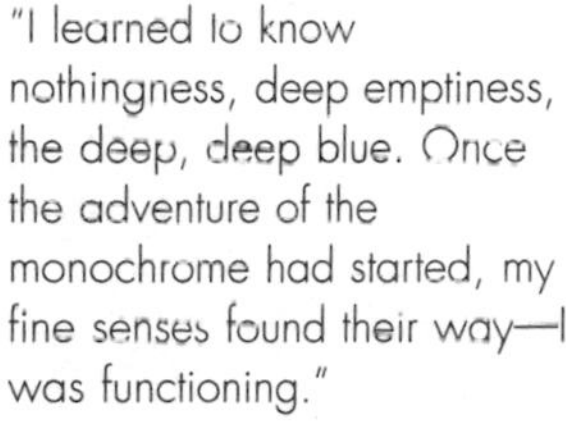

"I learned to know nothingness, deep emptiness, the deep, deep blue. Once the adventure of the monochrome had started, my fine senses found their way—I was functioning."

—**Yves Klein**

"We represented something people hadn't thought about for years. Even hippies hated us, and it's hard to get a hippie to hate anything."

—**Alice Cooper**

"Artists knock on silence for answering music. They pursue meaninglessness until they can force it to mean."

—**Rollo May**

"Sometimes when I am writing, I am aware of a rhythm, a dance, a fury, which is as yet empty of words."

—**Stephen Spender**

■ *I sense that meaning sparks illuminate my path, however mysteriously, and serve to build up my immunity to viral attacks of meaninglessness. I will prize the meaning sparks that ignite from the repeated encounters of my consciousness with the world.*

Meaninglessness

"If you gaze long into an abyss, the abyss will gaze back into you."

—Friedrich Nietzsche

"The dignity of man lies in his ability to face reality in all its meaninglessness."

—Martin Esslin

"God made everything out of nothing. But the nothingness shows through."

—Paul Valéry

"The farce is finished. I go to seek a vast perhaps."

—François Rabelais

Artists are built to care about meaning and to decide for themselves what is meaningful and what is not. But since they accept no ready-made meanings, it is their lot to fall prey to disturbing episodes of meaninglessness. These episodes are real and painful: while they persist, an artist is neither motivated nor anchored. But meaning is renewable: the artist rises, steps out into the sun, sees the rock to be chiseled and the spectacle of life, and feels the return of his reasons for being.

■ *When meaninglessness strikes I will make new meaning. I may be no stranger to despair, alienation, and other meaning drains, but I also know how to recharge my batteries: through art, through love, through play, through intimacy with the mysteries and beauties that surround me.*

Memory

Artists possess a special sort of memory. They remember vibrations and fleeting images, the look of a film they loved and the feel of beautiful passages from their favorite book. But everyday living clouds an artist's ability to remember; the past becomes lost in a too-fractured present. If an artist can quiet herself, those all-important memories will have a chance to resurface. Then she may capture the essence of her past, the fruit of her experience, and deepen her art with her memories.

"In 1973, I set my brain back to 1915 and I managed to remember flowers—and paint them—as I had seen them then. Quite a feat. And the flowers were fresher."

—**Alice Neel**

"The most vital things in the look of a landscape endure only for a moment. Work should be done from memory: memory of that vital moment."

—**Robert Henri**

"The Lake is with me today. The memory of a feeling. And when I feel that thing, I want to paint it."

—**Joan Mitchell**

"Own only what you can always carry with you: let your memory be your travel bag."

—**Aleksandr Solzhenitsyn**

■ *I will dare to remember. If a past failure or tragedy floods into memory, I may have to grieve and work to recover my balance; but such blows will not prevent me from cultivating and encouraging my memory. My memory is the library of my experiences: I will read there avidly.*

Miracles

"When I start drawing an ordinary thing I realize how extraordinary it is, what a sheer miracle: the branching of a tree, the structure of a dandelion's seed puff."

—**Frederick Franck**

"I know a lot of people didn't expect our relationship to last—but we just celebrated our two-month anniversary."

—**Britt Ekland**

"I produce music as an apple tree produces apples."

—**Camille Saint-Saëns**

"Everything is miraculous. It is a miracle that one does not melt in one's bath."

—**Pablo Picasso**

An artist believes in everyday miracles. Life is a miracle; his medium is miraculous; the universe of asteroids and breadfruit, human nature and the smell of the tropics is an utterly mysterious accomplishment. But as disappointments mount and the struggle to survive intensifies, an artist is apt to lose his taste for miracles. The world takes on a dull sheen and nothing strikes his palate as special. But if the weary artist can only rekindle his sense of hope, he will see that the miraculous still surrounds him everywhere.

■ *I am a miracle. To honor my own amazing existence, I will live like a wonder and a marvel. I will do work that teases the truth out of the air and seduces an indifferent cosmos into caring. I will cause my miraculous fellow human beings to get up and dance, and I will dance with them!*

MISTAKES

We do not want our doctors or accountants to make mistakes, but we surely expect our artists to make them. A writer will not see his way in the story, and may misstep badly; a bass player will get nervous for an instant and play the wrong chord in front of ten thousand people. An accident might be blamed on fate, on a bad batch of paint, or a computer glitch: but for mistakes we get to take the credit. The artist who hopes to eliminate mistakes will discover himself completely blocked; the master artist sighs and says, "I will make mistakes as a matter of course."

"A life spent in making mistakes is not only more honorable but more useful than a life spent doing nothing."

—GEORGE BERNARD SHAW

"My idea of composition is to spoil as much manuscript paper as possible."

—GUSTAV HOLST

"A doctor can bury his mistakes but an architect can only advise his client to plant vines."

—FRANK LLOYD WRIGHT

"Man must strive and, in striving, must go wrong."

—JOHANN WOLFGANG VON GOETHE

■ *I will make mistakes. Every mistake will hurt at least a little; when I ruin something in which I've invested a lot, I will weep. But to be an artist is to make mistakes. I know that; I accept that. To reduce the number of mistakes I make, I will master my craft; if I fear making mistakes, I will overcome that fear. Mistakes are part of my landscape.*

MOODS

"We moan about not working; and if we get a job we moan about the director, the script, and the reviews. If the play's a hit, we moan about the long run ahead of us. Then we moan because the play closes and we're out of work."

—**DEREK JACOBI**

"The creative person finds himself in a state of turmoil, restlessness, emptiness, and unbearable frustration unless he expresses his inner life in some creative way."

—**SILVANO ARIETI**

"One must be pitiless about this matter of 'mood.' In a sense, the writing will *create* the mood."

—**JOYCE CAROL OATES**

"The birds' song gets on my nerves. I feel like trampling every worm."

—**PAUL KLEE**

In whose control are an artist's moods? If she means to sculpt or play the flute but isn't in the mood, what will she do? If she feels sad, agitated, and lonely, must that keep her from her art? Artists must avoid using their moods as excuses: if an artist is grim, let her lighten her mood or else work grimly. If she is lonely, let her first toil at her art and then merrily search for a playmate. Artists will want to better master their moods, or else their moods will master them.

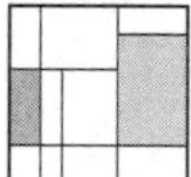

■ *I know that my black moods, angry moods, and upset moods cost me weeks and months of peace and productivity. I will gain some control over my moods, for the sake of my art, my life, and my loved ones. I refuse to let my moods cripple and thwart me.*

MUSIC

Music needs no explanations. But if music is simple it is simple in the way life itself is simple. A songwriter may write a hundred ordinary songs before writing one that makes you want to listen to her; she can't explain the rightness of that special one any more than she can explain the wrongness of the others. How was it that she labored so hard on those, boring herself and fooling herself, and then had her song of songs just flow through her? No doubt some simple thing happened—nothing but the marriage of long learning and deep letting-go, for which every artist lives.

"After silence, that which comes nearest to expressing the inexpressible is music."

—**Aldous Huxley**

"What is best in music is not to be found in the notes."

—**Gustav Mahler**

"Music must be an evidence for living."

—**Toshiro Mayuzumi**

"Music is the fragrance of the universe."

—**Giuseppe Mazzini**

"Music is an outburst of the soul."

—**Frederick Delius**

■ *Sometimes the art I create is like silence in a vaster silence. But sometimes it is symphonic—or jazzy, bluesy, rocking. I will be a master musician, alive to rhythm and melody, able to invest in my graphics or stage plays the voice of the oboe and the cello, the clay flute and the singer. I am a music maker.*

each has its own beauty

MYSTERY

"Once I'm writing, something mysterious happens. Something beyond explanation—not so much an escape from reality as a confrontation with a deeper reality."

—**Ellen Taaffe Zwilich**

"There is a mysterious identity of essence between the principle of the theater and that of alchemy."

—**Antonin Artaud**

"My aim in painting is to create pulsating, luminous, and open surfaces that emanate a mystic light, in accordance with my deepest insight into the experience of life and nature."

—**Hans Hofmann**

"The job of the artist is always to deepen the mystery."

—**Francis Bacon**

Sometimes things are inexplicable. Sometimes things are explicable, but so very beautifully that the elegance of their explication is its own mystery. How could cellos, bassoons, and flutes have come to be, and why should their singing together move a person to tears? How can pigment on canvas have the power to entice a person to devote a whole life to painting? Mystery is the artist's first subject of study, her best subject—even her only subject.

■ *When something is clear, it is clear, and I am the first to say so. But how much mystery still remains after that! I am mysterious; the earth is mysterious; every particle of the universe is mysterious. That mystery is simply everywhere fills me with passion and inspiration.*

Nature

Our ancestors more intimately related to nature than do artists of today. But that an artist can't pick her own medicinal herbs or that she rejects plein air painting hardly means that her heart isn't connected to the natural world. Still, she must find in these modern times the concrete ways of making that connection meaningful. Does she need to keep good brown earth in her pockets? Grow green onions in a corner of her studio? Meditate on the ants on her windowsill for the sake of her next ballet? However she does it, she will want to invite nature to visit.

"The observation of nature is part of an artist's life. It enlarges his form knowledge, keeps him fresh, and feeds inspiration."

—**Henry Moore**

"The Louvre is a good book to consult but it must only be an intermediary. The real and immense study that must be taken up is the manifold picture of nature."

—**Paul Cézanne**

"A love of nature is a consolation against failure."

—**Berthe Morisot**

"My soul can find no staircase to Heaven unless it be through Earth's loveliness."

—**Michelangelo**

■ *A part of nature myself, I need to see the sky, hear the songs of birds, watch the mountains changing colors. These rejuvenate me; these make me better. As much as I must dwell in my mind, still I must make time to abide with nature and expose my animal skin to the elements.*

NETWORKING

"People often ask me how I find writers. I dig, I ask, I listen, I look. When I get to know a writer, I'm never bashful. I get on the phone and ask, 'What have you written lately?' "

—**JUDY COLLINS**

"An actor needs success in order to get opportunities to be good, so he concentrates on achieving success, and in the process he may lose whatever it is that has made him good."

—**BEN GAZZARA**

"Fashions, after all, are only induced epidemics."

—**GEORGE BERNARD SHAW**

"In business, contacts are the name of the game. Why, in the art world, are they considered dirty?"

—**BRETT SINGER**

Many artists pay too little attention to business relationships and some pay too much. Is it really wise not to contact that agent who's a friend of your roommate, what with a completed novel sitting in your drawer? On the flip side, is attending another social event really the thing to do, when you haven't worked on your screenplay for months? Striking a balance between solitary work and socializing is an art in its own right; and networking is a duty an artist dare not forsake out of revulsion or pride.

■ *I will improve my networking skills. I will build useful, cordial business relationships. Whether I want to or not, I will network. I don't intend to become a social butterfly, squandering my time and energy; but if I want an audience and a career, I had better make personal contacts in the marketplace.*

Neurosis

What exactly is mental health? Who is well and who is sick? Is the patriotic conformist who spanks his child the well one? Is the anxious artist who struggles with boredom and depression the sick one? Let us trot out the word *neurosis* only if we mean to use it lovingly: the "neurotic" is a person in pain, besieged by existential panics, overvigilant and insecure. There is no high place from which to look down on our anxious brothers and sisters: we are all obliged to seek out a cure for what ails us.

"Kierkegaard was once asked, 'What is a poet?' He answered that a poet was an unhappy man whose moans and cries of anguish were transformed into ravishing music."

—**Langdon Gilkey**

"What marks the artist is his power to shape the material of the pain we all have."

—**Lionel Trilling**

"Perhaps someday everyone will have neurosis."

—**Vincent van Gogh**

"It is not work that kills men; it is worry. Worry is rust upon the blade."

—**Henry Ward Beecher**

■ *My anxieties are real afflictions. How can I reduce their terrible potency? The things that I do as an artist—taking risks, maintaining consciousness, handling criticism and rejection—surely do not reduce that anxiety. But I am not attached to my "neurosis": I will make it my job to learn to live less nervously.*

No-Saying

"The only power an actor has is the ability to say no."

—**Kathleen Turner**

"Resistance to tyrants is obedience to God."

—**Thomas Jefferson**

"No morality can be founded on authority, even if the authority were divine."

—**A. J. Ayer**

"A country with no anarchists is a finished country. I am an anarchist."

—**Arletty**

"All great truths begin as blasphemies."

—**George Bernard Shaw**

What if the director exclaims, "I want you for this role!"—but the movie is a horrible, exploitative mess? The artist takes a deep breath and replies, "No, thank you." What if the gallery owner says, "I'd love to hang your new work—but I get eighty percent"? The artist blinks and whispers, "No, I don't think so." The artist would love to say "yes" always, because so few chances come his way: and still he must sometimes say no, in order to be able to respect himself.

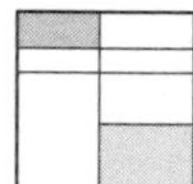

■ *Because of the nature of the business I'm in, because of the fierce competition and the limited opportunities, I am loath to say no to anyone. But I will act with integrity, even in the face of the profound pulls I feel to say yes: I affirm that I have the magnificent word "No!" available to me.*

Nonconformity

The person who deviates from the norm has good reasons to feel frightened. In one country she will be studiously ignored, in another country she will be executed. Why then not just conform? Because to conform means to not think, to not love, to not live. Nonconformity is the dangerous but correct stance of the self-respecting artist, who makes up her own mind and then speaks it. To walk within the lines, in order to meet the demands of the marketplace or to have civil relationships, is one thing; but to keep silent in the face of an evil one plainly sees is quite another.

"The writer is the only surviving individualist in a mass age. To his orthodox contemporaries he seems a semi-madman."

—**Boris Pasternak**

"The greater part of what my neighbors call good I believe in my soul to be bad."

—**Henry David Thoreau**

"It does not matter how badly you paint, just so long as you don't paint badly like other people."

—**George Edward Moore**

"Minorities are the stars of the firmament; majorities, the darkness in which they float."

—**Martin Fischer**

■ *I can conform, if need be; I understand the rules and realities of my universe. But still I am a nonconformist. I will choose my battles carefully, but I will choose them—I am the rebel, the radical, the hero, the real misfit, the one whose life and art will make a difference.*

Nostalgia

very good

"Today must not be a souvenir of yesterday, and so the struggle is everlasting. Who am I today? What do I see today? How shall I *use* what I know, and how shall I avoid being victim of what I know? Life is not repetition."

—**Robert Henri**

"There's a lot of landscape I never would have described if I hadn't been homesick. The impulse was nostalgia."

—**Joan Didion**

"Every act of rebelling expresses a nostalgia for innocence."

—**Albert Camus**

"I am still searching for the expression of those confused sensations that we bring with us at birth."

—**Paul Cézanne**

Nostalgia is an integral part of human nature. We write in part because we are nostalgic for the feelings we once had, sitting in a sunny corner reading a masterwork. We are nostalgic for the happy endings fairy tales provided. We are nostalgic for summer days, darkened theaters, cherry ices. But our job is to bring the enduring, unsentimental past into the present, where it can inform our art and guide us into the future, rather than hanker too much for what is gone and perhaps never was.

■ *To live unnostalgically is to invite in an existential coldness that I can hardly tolerate. But still my job is to discover what is true for today and tomorrow, not what was sweet and soothing yesterday. Waves of nostalgia will sometimes flood over me: but each time I will swim back to the shore of the present.*

Opportunities

Often the artist has more in her than her circumstances allow her to reveal. She could dance the lead in a brilliant new ballet—but either the ballet does not exist, or the role is not offered to her. She could make a fifty-hour documentary on a subject that excites her—but where will the money come from, and who will publicize and distribute it? It is a hard truth that a capable artist may only occasionally be offered work as large as she is. But it is her job to seek that large work out, by assiduously making contacts in the marketplace, in her role as self-promoter and self-advocate.

"What I am looking for is a masterpiece. I don't want to waste my time. I am tired of experiments."

—**Natalia Makarova**

"Hollywood can't contain a great talent, because even the best films aren't enough to nurture that kind of talent."

—**Kim Stanley**

"Ability is of little account without opportunity."

—**Napoleon Bonaparte**

"I feel that the greatest reward for doing is the opportunity to do more."

—**Jonas Salk**

■ *Probably I will amass far fewer chances to demonstrate my capacities than I would like. But I will keep searching out the best opportunities; and I will devise ways—by joining with others, by reinventing the universe—to create new opportunities for myself and others.*

ORGANIZATION

"Once you concentrate on organizing, ideas fall into place with an almost audible click."

—JANE HARRIGAN

"We work not only to produce but to give value to time."

—EUGÈNE DELACROIX

"Sanity is perhaps the ability to punctuate."

—PARRY IDRIS

"The triumph of anything is a matter of organization."

—KURT VONNEGUT

An artist does not organize her calendar, studio, notes, thoughts, and life for the sake of organization. Indeed, she may be inclined to resist organization on principle, on the principle that to stop to contain the chaos just for the sake of neatness is a waste of her precious time. True enough: but the dangers of disorganization are themselves profound. Can she really do everything she means to do—her art and her art business, her loving relating, her work inside herself and her work outside—without some careful organization?

■ *I will become organized. To that end I will take stock and see what organization I really need. I will not stop at straightening my desk, but will better organize my thoughts and more clearly envision the great work I mean to do. I will risk reorganizing the pieces that comprise the puzzle of my life.*

Originality

Creativity often is defined as the ability to produce new and novel things. But this is a limited view of the matter. As a by-product of the process of creating, the artist will often produce new things, but what is going on inside him is not a hunger for novelty. Rather he is gnawing on a problem—chewing, sweating, and struggling—in order to find its true solution. If nothing "original" comes of that gnawing, the work can still have great merit. Was Einstein unoriginal because a unified field theory eluded him?

"Know your own bone; gnaw at it, bury it, unearth it, and gnaw it still."

—**Henry David Thoreau**

"One machine can do the work of fifty ordinary men. No machine can do the work of one extraordinary man."

—**Elbert Hubbard**

"The merit of originality is not novelty; it is sincerity."

—**Thomas Carlyle**

"I really do not aim at any originality."

—**Wolfgang Amadeus Mozart**

■ *I will not worry about originality as an abstract idea. I will simply work deeply and honestly, challenging myself, choosing great problems, learning and loving, and striving to bring my heart, mind, and muscles to bear on the largest themes. I am an original and will work like one.*

Painting

"Every artist dips his brush in his own soul, and paints his own nature into his pictures."

—Henry Ward Beecher

"Lines, surfaces, and volumes are only nuances of the notion of fullness."

—Jean Metzinger

"There is a sort of elation about sunlight on the upper part of a house."

—Edward Hopper

"Once a mere collection, the art museum is by way of becoming a sort of shrine, the only one of the modern age."

—André Malraux

The painter in every artist has a tactile sense, a color sense, strong feelings about shape and form, and a connection to line. An artist's sense of formal balance allows him to intuitively know that the heads in a room form an ellipse, even though his medium is drumming or dancing. These loves and intuitions are what the artist brings to his poetry or filmmaking, his music video or choreography. To imagine that painting is only about pigment on canvas is to forget what we learn and relearn every day: that imagery is the stuff of our thoughts and our dreams.

■ *Whatever my medium, however I am to be an artist, I can learn from O'Keeffe and van Gogh, from Rembrandt and Matisse. I can see, feel, and dream like a painter; I can bring a painterly texture to my next song and a painterly look to my next film. I am a visual artist.*

Patience

Patience is not only a virtue: it is so necessary that its absence will doom an artist. An "impatient novelist," an "impatient sculptor," an "impatient violinist" must grow frustrated and unhappy. How much patience is required to parent children? To wait for the flowering of things that do not bloom until the springtime? An artist can feel impatient stalled at the checkout counter if she likes: but with regard to her work she must maintain a deep, abiding patience.

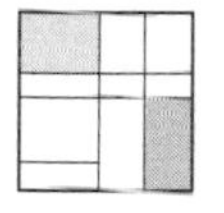

"In the evening I go up in the desert and spend hours watching the sun go down, just enjoying it, and every day I go out and watch it again. I draw some and there is a little painting and so the days go by."

—Georgia O'Keeffe

"Sometimes you have the feeling that some little imp is standing behind you and dictating to you, but he gives it to you slowly, drop by drop."

—Isaac Bashevis Singer

"I devoted myself simply to being a solitary person entrusted with a specific task."

—Jacobo Timerman

"There is no nature in an instant."

—A. N. Whitehead

■ *I revere patience. I know how impatient I can be, how overwrought and anxious I can get: but I pledge to do a better job of calming my nerves and regaining my balance. I will become a more controlled whirlwind: for the sake of my art, I will really learn patience.*

Performance Art

"The best thing about the term 'performance artist' is that it includes just about everything you might want to do."

—**Laurie Anderson**

"There is no strong performance without a little fanaticism in the performer."

—**Ralph Waldo Emerson**

"The attraction of the virtuoso for the public is very like that of the circus for the crowd. There is always the hope that something dangerous will happen."

—**Claude Débussy**

"Listening to this screaming music for a minute or two, one conjures up an orchestra of madmen, sexual maniacs, led by a man-stallion beating time with an enormous phallus."

—**Maxim Gorky**

Didn't the troubadours transform their world, and ours, with their vision of romantic love? What revolution might a performance artist undertake today? Might he appear out of nowhere with a new idea and proclaim it from his roving pulpit? Mirror himself to let passersby reflect on their humanity? Infiltrate the media, take his act into corporate America, play politician and run for office, play cleric and form a religion? The free, unfettered performance artist can do any silly, wise thing that tickles his fancy.

■ *Have I thought of myself as a performance artist? Well, perhaps I will! Perhaps I will be a poet-singer, a prose-actor, a startling public player who brings his art out from solitary confinement and into the teeming streets. Maybe I will make some new friends and enemies! I think I will try on the hat of performance artist, to see how I like the fit.*

Persistence

Who wouldn't give up? Another dozen canvases ruined. Another year without a decent-paying role. Another novel that never quite came alive. Another band self-destructing. Another ten auditions and nothing; another twenty query letters and nothing; another fruitless round of mailing out slides. Who wouldn't give up? Only the persistent artist. She lives through all this and by so doing retains the chance of becoming the exception.

"When I was just starting out in Chicago, someone told me, if you make ten calls a day you are bound to get work. I made twenty."

—**Sam Grey**

"Keep spiritually sound and be persistent. Persistence is the key. Just never stop believing in your dream."

—**Deborah Aquila**

"The saints are the sinners who keep on going."

—**Robert Louis Stevenson**

"I never wrote anything that was published until I was forty."

—**James Michener**

■ *Can I be Hercules? Can I meet all these challenges, survive these long odds, run this painful gauntlet? Will my heart harden and my mind break? I do need the strength of a god! But if that's the strength I need, then I will become that god: persistent, heroic, magnificent.*

Personal Philosophy

"I am not a liberal, not a conservative, not a believer in gradual progress, not a monk. I should like to be a free artist and nothing more."

—**Anton Chekhov**

"Life is meaningless, cruel, stupid, and nevertheless magnificent—it does not make fun of man, but concerns itself with man no more than with the earthworm."

—**Hermann Hesse**

"People are starved for a way of life. They're hunting for a way to be or to act toward the world."

—**Sam Shepard**

"I prefer what is green to what is scorched."

—**Rosa Bonheur**

The artist, antagonistic to dogma, must invent her own personal philosophy from scratch. This is a difficult task that puts her at a disadvantage as life hurtles by her. "How," she broods, "can I be humane, honest, creative, and useful?" while around her people rush past, wondering no such things. But among the advantages she obtains are the following: her art is fresh and personal, her path is forever surprising, and her life is completely her own.

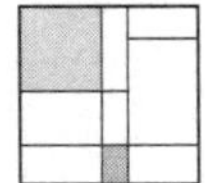

■ *I am responsible for constructing and maintaining my personal philosophy: if it is frayed or insufficient, I am the only one who can repair it. I will be my own Plato and Aristotle: I will know myself, guide myself, and be myself.*

Personality

Who is the architect of our personality? If personality is rigidly fixed at an early age, then unless we are formed plumb and level, we are doomed: let us reject that scenario. Let us say instead, My neighbor's character may be fixed, but that's his business: I am an artist, able to change my shape through my artistry. I can survey the structure that I am and add a porch or a skylight: if I can powerfully model clay or make my harp sing, can't I also make myself over in ways that please me?

"I was having trouble in school because of a combination of isolation and exhibitionism, grandiosity and depression."

—Jennifer Bartlett

"Every man has three characters—that which he exhibits, that which he has, and that which he thinks he has."

—Alphonse Karr

"Character is destiny."

—Heraclitus

"There's something in one's nature that is unchangeable; wherever one goes, it is always the dominating factor. You are born with a certain kind of sensibility, in relation to which you constantly react."

—Hans Hofmann

■ *If my personality needs alteration, I am the tailor to do the job. I will survey myself in the mirror; I will get out the needle and thread; I will cut the pattern and stitch together my new being. I have the power to change—and improve—my personality.*

Perspective

"At a distance this fine oak seems to be of ordinary size. But if I place myself under its branches, the impression changes completely: I see it as big, and even terrifying in its bigness."

—**Eugène Delacroix**

"It takes a certain maturity of mind to accept that nature works as steadily in rust as in rose petals."

—**Esther Warner Dendel**

"How many languages do we really speak?"

—**Alfredo Jaar**

"The reason for my painting large canvases is that I want to be intimate and human."

—**Mark Rothko**

What does a wall look like from an artist's perspective? Like a sculptural mass, evocative layers of peeling paint, a backdrop for his dance, a surface to play like a drum, a metaphor around which to build a poem: a thing entirely new because he has an artist's eyes. There is no "just" from an artist's perspective. Just a wheat field?—ask van Gogh. Just some bleached bones?—ask O'Keeffe. Just the same old mountain?—ask Cézanne. The tiniest speck is a galaxy, if your eyes are functioning.

■ *I have an artist's perspective. I will use my keen senses to navigate through life and to locate worthy projects to invest my heart in. If the world looks dull or uninviting from here, I can move and gain a new perspective: I am an artist and know all the vantage points.*

PHOTOGRAPHY

No artist should miss the experience of the darkroom, where images appear on paper so magically that for a second one doubts atheism. The chemical baths and ritual movements are less methods and tools of a trade than elements of a dance, a dance that takes light from the world, carries it into a private darkness, and enriches the world upon its return. The artist may never feel the urge to grip a camera, but the photograph—black-and-white, sepia-tinted, in blazing color—is part of her secret cache of loved things.

"Snow. White, white, white, soft and clean, and maddening shapes, with the whole world in them."

—ALFRED STIEGLITZ

"A photograph is a secret about a secret."

—DIANE ARBUS

"As structures are built, the photographer contrives new imagery that documents the encroachment of civilization."

—CHARLES TRAUB

"Sometimes I get to places just when God's ready to have somebody click the shutter."

—ANSEL ADAMS

■ *I am and always have been a camera. I possess snapshot memories; the art of photography resides in my being. I bring a knowledge of the differences between a black-and-white photograph and a color photograph to whatever art I make: I know when a pot must be gray, a poem blue, a song sun yellow. I have a photographer's heart and eye.*

POETRY

"You will not find poetry anywhere unless you bring some of it with you."

—**JOSEPH JOUBERT**

"Poetry is the art of substantiating shadows."

—**EDMUND BURKE**

"Why should it happen that among the great many women whom I see and am fond of, suddenly somebody I meet for half an hour opens the door into poetry?"

—**MAY SARTON**

"It is with words as with sunbeams—the more they are condensed, the deeper they burn."

—**ROBERT SOUTHEY**

We live most days too unpoetically. Our diet is thin, our mind troubled, our jaw set, our vision dark, the bedroom untidy, the traffic roaring: the beautiful seems bent on eluding us. How exactly can an artist add more poetry to her daily menu? Might she put a note on the refrigerator door: "More poetry, dear, more poetry!"? Versify first thing when she awakens? Create haiku in the spaces between worries? Each artist, born to poetry, still must seize the poetic out of her humdrum surroundings.

■ *I am a poet. I work in my favorite medium and am a poet in that medium. I am a poet in my relationships, a poet at my day job, a poet as I clean, cook, and change the oil. I bring poetry to a drab and weary world: this child of nursery rhymes has grown into a poet laureate.*

Possibility

Without meaning to, artists restrict their possibilities early on. They bite into one medium and that medium bites back; they become writers or sculptors forever. But twenty years later they may well look up and wonder, "Must I be just one kind of artist?" This is the disturbing but necessary question that artists are sometimes forced to ask themselves, if they are to keep up with their changing circumstances. Still, isn't it a small miracle that an artist retains the possibility of working with passion and love in any new medium of his choosing?

"Beyond useless discussions of figurative or abstract art is the imperious necessity to express oneself as one is, making ours all the energetic possibilities of the universe."

—**Antonio Saura**

"The whole sequence of evolution seems somehow to correspond to continued births, rebirths, and new births."

—**Otto Rank**

"All we are given are possibilities—to make ourselves one thing or another."

—**José Ortega y Gasset**

"Grace, or the Tao, surrounds us always. Whenever we are open to it for a moment, it enters into us."

—**Hermann Hesse**

■ *I have worked in one way for a long time now. I have written a great many poems; I have attended a great many band rehearsals. Today I will take a break and determine if a new thing is wanted. What is really true for me? What new door, guarding a world of rich possibility, would I like to open?*

POVERTY

"One of the most absurd questions I've heard asked is, 'But do you think he can handle a big budget?' Why should money be considered more difficult to handle than poverty?"

—**PETER BOGDANOVICH**

"Poverty is very good in poems, but very bad in practical life."

—**HENRY WARD BEECHER**

"For every talent that poverty has stimulated, it has blighted a hundred."

—**JOHN GARDNER**

"The line between hunger and anger is a thin line."

—**JOHN STEINBECK**

Artists rarely make a living at their art. Therefore an artist will experience poverty, unless he proves the rare exception or unless money appears from elsewhere. In order to preserve his sanity and honor his responsibilities, he has no choice but to make sense of his economic realities. Are any of his alternatives really palatable? Does he really want a second career or to be dependent on his mate? Does he really want anything but to fiddle or draw and be paid enough to live modestly? Whatever he may want, he must look reality in the eye and sharply calculate.

■ *As an artist dedicated to truth and beauty, it is likely that I will know poverty. But I do not accept poverty as my due: I affirm that I am entitled to all of life's riches. Despite the long odds, I will prove the exception: I will be the artist who lives creatively and can still pay his bills.*

Preparation

Creative work is first prepared for and only then realized. Improvisation requires preparation; spontaneity requires preparation. The very ability to approach a blank canvas or computer screen is contingent on the artist's inner preparations, contingent on the alignment of his heart, mind, and hands in the direction of his task. The artist who does not get ready will never be ready: an artist must prepare like any ardent apprentice to achieve mastery.

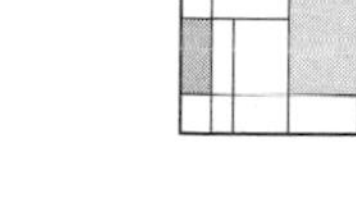

"We must never shirk the preparation in the wings, the practicing of the old self hypnotic act to transform ourselves completely before we step onto the stage."

—**Laurence Olivier**

"Confidence is preparation. Everything else is beyond your control."

—**Richard Kline**

"Luck is when preparation meets opportunity."

—**Oprah Winfrey**

"If I don't practice for one day, I know it; if I don't practice for two days, the critics know it; if I don't practice for three days, the audience knows it."

—**Ignacy Paderewski**

■ *I have not always been adequately prepared. Nor will I always be prepared in the future. But I understand the critical nature of preparation: I will do a better job of planning, readying, organizing, and rehearsing. I will start preparing myself right now for my next art encounter.*

PRESENT

"No artist is ahead of his time. He *is* his time. It is just that the others are behind the time."

—**MARTHA GRAHAM**

"Every work of art is the child of its time; each period produces an art of its own, which cannot be repeated."

—**WASSILY KANDINSKY**

"Real generosity toward the future consists in giving all to what is present."

—**ALBERT CAMUS**

"Eternity is a terrible thought. I mean, where is it going to end?"

—**TOM STOPPARD**

Because the present is unsettling, it's hardly a wonder that people, artists and nonartists alike, prefer to live in the past or the future. But an artist who lives in the past will do work insufficiently informed by the lifeblood of her own time: her work may be beautiful and even good, but will not ring true enough. And an artist who lives in the future, waiting for just the right moment to begin her work, will find her life slipping inexorably past. Every artist's solemn duty is to work right here, right now.

■ *Like anyone, I can let the present glide by me. But I am not happy that I possess such a talent. Isn't this exactly the right moment to be working? Isn't this exactly my unique time and place, completely worthy of my attention? I will inhabit this precise second of existence.*

PROBLEMS

Artists create their own problems and then fall in love with them. A boulder exists, a problem to no one: the artist decides that the boulder must yield up a family of reindeer. The writer's grandparents got divorced, but thirty long years ago: why is the artist still straining to understand that dissolution? Does this need to create problems make for a comfortable life? The artist can only chuckle. He may stand aghast at his own unyielding desire to set himself difficulties; but without them, he is bored and miserable.

"I see a flower. It gives me a sensation of the beautiful. I wish to paint it. And as soon as I wish to paint it I see the whole subject—flower—changed. It is now an art problem to resolve."

—**GEORGES VANTONGERLOO**

"Acting on the stage, you have the opportunity to go out there night after night and wrestle with the same problem. Even a writer doesn't have that kind of freedom."

—**GERALDINE PAGE**

"Life is not a spectacle or a feast; it is a predicament."

—**GEORGE SANTAYANA**

"You can chase a Beethoven symphony all your life and never catch up."

—**ANDRÉ PREVIN**

■ *My nature requires that I create or discover magnificent problems, which I must then attempt to solve as if my very life depended on their solution. That is how I am built; that is my glory and burden. I am a born problem-making, problem-seeking, and problem-solving creature.*

Products

"It is only when a pot comes from my wheel that I can reflect on its form, its beauty, and its meaning. One does and then one reflects."

—**Cecilia Davis Cunningham**

"Were I to begin life over again I would not hesitate to paint portraits cheap and slight, for the mass of folks can't judge the merits of a well-finished picture."

—**John Vanderlyn**

"Suchness transcends forms, but without depending on forms it cannot be realized."

—**Kukai**

"They're there, they're mine, they're my children."

—**Norman Mailer**

Artists are reluctant materialists. They make things, such as pots, novels, documentary films, sculptures, and albums of music, but consider them personal and precious, and not just commodities. But once made, all these things must take their place alongside the other ten thousand things of the world; they must compete in the world as products. Does an artwork lose its value to the artist because a price tag gets attached to it? Not if the artist affirms that his work is simultaneously a product like any other and also priceless.

■ *I am engaged in the making of precious things, which I will one day want to sell in the marketplace. I will make the transition from artist to salesperson easily, without balking or throwing fits: I can be artful in both the making and the selling.*

Prose

The word is every artist's tool. Articulateness is even a kind of cure for what ails us; a strong sentence a fine rebellion against meaninglessness; a stylish line a tidbit of happiness on a thin, sad day. The story the writer crafts, the speech the musician delivers in support of a worthy cause, the paragraph the sculptor polishes in order to provide her audience with a personal statement: in these loving ways every artist makes use of the word.

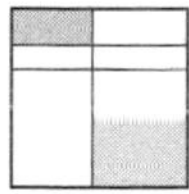

"Prose needs to be built like a cathedral. There one is truly without a name, without ambition, without help; on scaffoldings, alone with one's consciousness."

—**Rainer Maria Rilke**

"A story must be exceptional enough to justify its telling."

—**Thomas Hardy**

"A page of good prose seems to me the most serious dialogue that well-informed and intelligent men and women carry on today."

—**John Cheever**

"The good writer is not vague except when he has a reason."

—**Gary Provost**

■ *Language is a great deal—startling, powerful, profound, and miraculous—and I will manage it excellently. For the sake of expression, for the sake of my career, and for the sheer joy of it, I will fashion myself into a prose stylist.*

Public Art

"We are living in a state of emergency. I feel that more than ever we must step outside of the strictly art arena. It is not enough to make art."

—**Guillermo Gómez-Peña**

"Unlike much of what has previously been called public art, new-genre public art is based on engagement."

—**Suzanne Lacy**

"To search for the good and make it matter: this is the real challenge for the artist."

—**Estella Conwill Májozo**

"The work of art is a scream of freedom."

—**Christo**

There was a time when public art meant a bronzed war hero on the plaza. Today it means something radically different. Today it is the Vietnam Veterans Memorial, the living and the dead face-to-face for all eternity. Now it is ceremonial art, collective art, political art, environmental art. It is new-genre public art, the artist as aesthetician and activist, exploring her aliveness on the streets of her community.

■ *I am both a private artist and a public artist. I may not build monumental sculptures or transform the landscape, but I mean to live a less secretive and secluded life as an artist. If I am not precisely an activist, I am nevertheless an artist willing to be public, visible, and influential.*

Publicity

An artist's career depends on publicity. Whether that publicity is word of mouth or manufactured by a publicity machine, whether it is justified or contrived, whether it is a grassroots groundswell or a complete fabrication, there is no substitute for it: the artist who is not getting known is unknown. "I have a thing to sell" is a phrase each artist must come to embrace: for the survival of his work depends on press releases and advertisements, on radio, television, and newspaper coverage, on the trumpeting of the fact that it exists and is now available for purchase.

"We now sadly live in a country in which publicity has triumphed over culture."

—**Yale Udoff**

"Freedom! to spit in the eye of the passerby with advertising."

—**Aleksandr Solzhenitsyn**

"There is art—and there is advertising."

—**Albert Sterner**

"We are almost always totally deluded by the mythology of our particular period and place."

—**Pat Steir**

■ *I had not intended to publicize my wares: I had the idea that others would do that for me. But now I affirm that I will do my part to get my work known—the networking, the interviews, the tours, whatever is required—so that my art may receive the attention it deserves.*

REJECTION

"If nobody ever offers an opinion or takes the slightest interest in one's production, one loses not only all pleasure in them, but all power of judging their value."

—**FANNY MENDELSSOHN HENSEL**

"I've filled scrapbooks with rejection slips. I use them as coasters. Sometimes I have rejection parties."

—**LEE PENNINGTON**

"Man cannot remake himself without suffering."

—**ALEXIS CARREL**

"I feel much more creative now that I'm not carrying around that load of bitterness and despair because I was getting so little critical attention."

—**MAY SARTON**

From the point of view of the marketplace, there are innumerable reasons to reject an artist's work. It may be unpleasant, average, flawed, or difficult; the need for it may be slight or nonexistent; the artist may present his wares too anxiously or fail at the games the marketplace has invented. This is the short list: and everywhere artists' hearts are breaking. Even if he does a heroic job of recovering from rejection letter after rejection letter, an artist can't live on a steady diet of rejection: he must get his work wanted sometimes.

■ *I will get rejected. And I can stand rejection: but not in the absence of an occasional victory. I must and will have some successes. As great as the pain of rejection may be, I will risk inviting it by showing my art in the world; and to achieve the successes I need, I will do my best work and unravel the mysteries of the marketplace.*

RENAISSANCE

Even as the majority expresses its antipathy to art, we may be experiencing a renaissance. If you try to find it, it seems to vanish: and yet it is everywhere, in crowded bookstores, at the screening of documentaries, at monologue festivals, in music magazines bursting with band news. The savvy artist will search out and participate in this renaissance, even as it does its best to remain splendidly hidden.

"Only just now awakening after years of materialism, our soul is still infected with the despair born of unbelief, of lack of purpose and aim."

—**WASSILY KANDINSKY**

"We are in a renaissance now, but where are you going to find it?"

—**JOAN LITTLEWOOD**

"Exercising the social contract between the citizen and state, the artist works as citizen within the intimate spaces of community life."

—**YOLANDA LÓPEZ**

"We artists are mythmakers, and we participate with everybody else in the social construction of reality."

—**HELEN MAYER HARRISON**

■ *I feel more caught in a cultural blitzkrieg than engaged in cultural renewal. But maybe that is true only on the surface of things. Maybe good work is growing everywhere, in studios in the woods, in city centers, at the hands of millions of my fellow artists. I will join the renaissance that just may be blooming all around me.*

REPETITION

"This apple tree is not the first one I draw, but perhaps the thousandth. I feel the sap rise to its spreading branches. I feel in my toes how its roots grip the earth."

—**FREDERICK FRANCK**

"There are only two or three human stories, and they go on repeating themselves as fiercely as if they had never happened before."

—**WILLA CATHER**

"If you approach every character in the same way, you'll probably end up playing them all in the same way."

—**PAMELA REED**

"To copy oneself is pathetic."

—**PABLO PICASSO**

Because certain vistas, keys, or stories interest him forever, because the mastery of his medium is based on practice and more practice, an artist will indeed repeat himself. But there are also less admirable reasons for retracing one's footsteps. If he repeats himself solely because the marketplace demands it, or because he is afraid to take risks, or because he is too busy or tired to use his imaginative faculties, then "repetition" gives off a foul odor. Either a master or a hack may repeat himself.

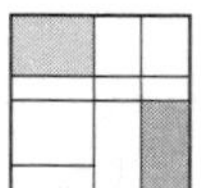

■ *Like everyone, I repeat myself. But in what sense is that a problem? Am I really bored and taking it too easy? Am I stuck on one note? Or is the repetition I'm engaged in vital to the development of my art? I must know: when I see that I am repeating myself, I will stop and find out why.*

Responsibility

Like everyone, artists sometimes tend to avoid their responsibilities. But they do so with no devilish glee. Their irresponsible acts fill them with guilt and revulsion. An artist knows when she's abandoned her book and done it an injustice; failed, out of hopelessness and fatigue, to audition for a part that suits her; or avoided finishing her mural out of fear she will ruin it. Let each artist take stock anew and better meet her own standards.

"I must take responsibility for my work. That word may be grandiose, but there's an ethic involved in creation."

—**Cecilia Davis Cunningham**

"The hottest places in Hell are reserved for those who in time of great moral crises maintain their neutrality."

—**Dante Alighieri**

"The moral dimension of language must be brought out. All good writers are sworn enemies of complacency and dogma."

—**Barry Lopez**

"One of the strains of going to the theater each night is bearing your responsibility to the author and the other actors."

—**Paul Newman**

■ *I mean to be a responsible person: I take responsibility for my life and my art. I am in charge of polishing my screenplay, selling my graphics, arriving at the theater with my part memorized. I renew my pledge to act ethically and responsibly.*

"A mind too active is no mind at all."

—**Theodore Roethke**

"I do not think that obsession is funny or that not being able to stop one's intensity is funny."

—**Jim Dine**

"To do great work a man must be very idle as well as very industrious."

—**Samuel Butler**

"Often nothing good is accomplished at the first attack. One takes a rest; and then all of a sudden the decisive idea presents itself to the mind."

—**Henri Poincaré**

No one can take up residence on Mercury; no one can live underwater; and no one can obsess constantly, pressured and pursued by her thoughts, tortured by an intense anxiety, without risking meltdown. How many days running can an artist put in twenty-hour stints in the studio? How many book ideas can a writer pursue simultaneously? How many days on the road can a performer manage? Artists must toil and obsess: but they must also manufacture their own shutdown systems, their own ways of giving the body and brain a rest.

■ *Obsessing about my work and lavishing great energy on it are dangerous necessities. I must monitor myself carefully: I will not be a shooting star that burns up and vaporizes. I will take the good rests I need, long before I find myself on the verge of a breakdown.*

REVIEWS

If office workers had pundits review their job performance on television or in the newspapers, suicide and homicide rates would skyrocket. But artists are supposed to take their public floggings gracefully, without a second thought or a single dish smashed. Really, how natural is that? So unnatural as to help explain why artists are wounded, deeply and even permanently, by the reviews they receive. The wise artist recognizes reviews as special land mines in the art world minefield: he considers them, learns from them, ignores them, and survives them.

"An actor can remember his briefest notice long after he has forgotten his phone number and where he lives."

—**JEAN KERR**

"What is reviewmanship? It is how to be one-up on the author without actually tampering with the text."

—**STEPHEN POTTER**

"If I believed what they wrote, I'd have slit my wrists a long time ago."

—**WILLIAM GOLDMAN**

"You're there to be shot at, and that's part of it."

—**NORMAN MAILER**

■ *I want reviews, for to be reviewed is to be known. Therefore I accept the negative reviews along with the positive ones. While I can't help being affected by them, I will nevertheless maintain my sense of balance. No review, however flattering, will turn my head; and no review, however scathing, will destroy me.*

Risk-Taking

"I can recall disapproving as a child of the golden mean, always thinking there was more to be learned from the dark journey."

—**Joan Didion**

"I have never liked the middle ground—the most boring place in the world."

—**Louise Nevelson**

"No noble thing can be done without risks."

—**Michel Eyquem de Montaigne**

"During every really creative act, the artist finds himself homeless. To overcome this state he has to call up his last reserves of strength."

—**Asger John**

What risks must artists take? The first is to risk proclaiming unequivocally, "I am an artist." The second is to risk making every manner of mistake, hundreds and thousands of them. The third . . . but the list is very long. Who wouldn't prefer a little safety, a little ease to all this risk-taking? To risk day after day and decade after decade is a difficult, nerve-racking business, capable of bruising the strongest ego. But this is the artist's path, which he embraces even with a certain zest.

■ *How brave am I? I hardly know. Sometimes I flee from danger; sometimes I hold my ground. Sometimes I cower; sometimes I stand erect. Certainly I am not always a risk-taking creature. But to be the artist I mean to be, I will take at least a few necessary risks each and every day.*

Routine

Productive artists just do their work. They work on the book they are working on; when that book is done, they work on the next one. If an artist can establish a routine—if she can exorcise her demons and love herself enough so that each day she finds the wherewithal to start—then she can canalize her wildness into the creation of a body of work. Despite her doubts and distractions, a brave artist will routinely approach her work each new day, as naturally as she breathes and stretches.

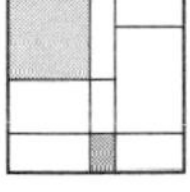

"Neurotic people or alcoholics make better copy, and people talk about them, tell anecdotes about them. The quiet people just do their work."

—Joyce Carol Oates

"There is a time for the labor of digging and mixing earths, a time for the heat of fire, and a time for contemplating what is done."

—Cecilia Davis Cunningham

"Writing every day is wonderful."

—Maria Irene Fornes

"If I don't paint for one day, I don't feel well physically or mentally."

—Raphael Soyer

■ *I have not always followed a routine. Nor do I even much like the idea. But I wonder if that dislike isn't related to anxiety and avoidance tactics. I will reconsider the matter of routine: I will create a routine, follow it, and embrace it if it serves me.*

Savoring

"I arise in the morning torn between a desire to save the world and a desire to savor the world. That makes it hard to plan the day."

—E. B. White

"The geometer measures, the painter savors."

—Jean Metzinger

"Adopt the pace of nature."

—Ralph Waldo Emerson

"Dawn itself is the most neglected masterpiece of the modern world."

—R. Murray Schafer

Artists are built to savor the world, but they are also built to save it. Can an artist stare long hours at the sky, drinking it in, or must he busy himself with the good deeds he has assigned himself? Can he play his clay flute for his own enjoyment, or must he turn his attention to world affairs and local elections? Or is the answer that he do both, making time for savoring and time for saving? Or even both at once, creating art that is both galvanizing and graceful?

■ *I am a creature made to fully enjoy my senses and to bask in intellectual pleasures. I savor my solitude, the spring air, the strangeness of human relationships. Savoring is so valuable to me that I will go so far as to make myself over: I will achieve better balance just to give myself the opportunity to savor life more.*

Sculpture

When we studied mass and density in physics, they perhaps left us unmoved. But no big rock has ever left a child unaltered. No mountain, no little mound of earth, no twig on the ground, no spire, no street lamp, no lamb in the morning mist, if observed, fails to awaken our own humanity. If this is strange and inexplicable, let us still honor it, and remind ourselves that the sculptor's art is there to educate any willing artist.

"The place for a sculpture is found by walking."

—**Richard Long**

"Gravity is my favorite form creator."

—**Claes Oldenburg**

"If light things are handled as if they're heavy, and heavy things as if they're weightless, one finds an almost complete control over nature, instead of being dominated by it."

—**Isamu Noguchi**

"A large piece of stone or wood placed almost anywhere at random in a field, orchard, or garden immediately looks right and inspiring."

—**Henry Moore**

■ *I may not work in basalt or steel, but I am a sculptor. I fabricate with words, build impasto ridges, create mass with guitars and drums. I let gravity inform my stage sets, make mobiles of my dancers. Even without a chisel or a blowtorch, I am a master sculptor.*

Self-Criticism

"I hate to see myself on the screen. I hate the way I look. I hate the sound of my voice. I'm always thinking I should have played it better."

—**Elizabeth Taylor**

"My verses are no damn good."

—**Dorothy Parker**

"I can pardon everyone's mistakes but my own."

—**Cato the Elder**

"The further I go, the sorrier I am about how little I know: it is this that bothers me the most."

—**Claude Monet**

The sincere artist rarely pardons his own mistakes, even though he would love to be less self-critical. Part of him argues, "Let me relax and accept mediocrity, just like the next guy!" Part of him counters, "No, I must demand the best from myself, and then punish myself when I fall short!" So the merry artist gets to criticize himself coming and going: first for taking life seriously, and then for not measuring up.

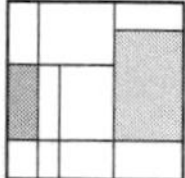

■ *I recognize how quickly I rush to chastise myself for all my shortcomings, all the mistakes I make, all the opportunities I miss. But this self-criticism only blocks me and saddens me terribly. So I will be done with it! I am tired of whipping myself: I prefer hard work and exaltation to self-criticism.*

Self-Deception

How can an artist be both so clear-eyed and so blind? How can she delve deeply into human affairs in her novel and not see that she is ignoring her children? How can she memorize an opera and not remember how to love? How can she draw a bird's intricate wing but not draw sensible conclusions about the details of her own life? Artists must learn to use their profound skills first of all in better understanding their predicament and in practicing less self-deception.

"The folly of mistaking oneself for an oracle is built right into us."

—Paul Valéry

"A writer judging his own work is like a deceived husband—he is frequently the last person to appreciate the true state of affairs."

—Robert Traver

"It is in the ability to deceive oneself that the greatest talent is shown."

—Anatole France

"It may be that the deep necessity of art is the examination of self-deception."

—Robert Motherwell

■ *If I am deceiving myself, how will I know it? Just by trying: for self-knowledge is also in the human repertoire. Do I have some suspicions about the ways in which I am deceiving myself? I will honor and examine those suspicions; I will see through the tricks I am pulling on myself and put a stop to them.*

SELF-DESTRUCTION

"I made a wasteland out of everything I touched."

—**RAYMOND CARVER**

"When an attractive but aloof man comes along, there are some of us who offer to shine his shoes with our underpants."

—**LYNDA BARRY**

"I have had just about all I can take of myself."

—**S. N. BEHRMAN**

"Artistic temperament sometimes seems a battleground, a dark angel of destruction and a bright angel of creativity wrestling."

—**MADELEINE L'ENGLE**

Every moment that we are not secure in our understanding of our job—to be humane, to love ourselves and to love others, to do work that is beautiful, true, and good—is a moment we can enter a hell of misadventures and self-disgust. Is it enough to paint well and then get drunk? To star in a hit drama and each night go hunting for heroin? To play the piano beautifully but be filled with rage and hate? Self-destruction is no charming game: an artist must consider his life worth saving and then save it.

■ *Can I rid myself of the despair that makes me careless and self-destructive? Somehow I must. Can I stop this slide that is ruining my talents, my organs, my life? I must! I must locate a last drop of self-love and turn sharply in the direction of self-preservation and renewal.*

SENTIMENTALITY

Audiences tend to demand sentimental work. They want songs that come nicely home, stories that end happily, movies that uplift, images that soothe. They want a composer's melodies, not his spiritual struggles; the allure of film, not its bite. Since the paying customer wants his reality delivered in sugarcoated, bite-sized pieces, the truth-telling artist stands perplexed: should she do what is right or opt for the sentimental alternative?

"I reject somber Jewish painting, with its literary, religious, and philosophical symbols. I feel that the use of Jewish symbols is merely a way of exploiting sentiment."

—YEHESKIEL STREICHMAN

"Most writers become sentimental or overly romantic when they're writing about a woman, and that makes it difficult for an actress."

—KIM HUNTER

"The true artist views nature from his own time. The hostile audience views nature in the rosy past."

—DAVID SMITH

"A sentimentalist is simply one who desires to have the luxury of an emotion without paying for it."

—OSCAR WILDE

■ *It is a painfully real problem that audiences demand sentimental work. It is a second considerable problem that too often I am tempted by sentimentality myself. But I will not sentimentalize the truth: I will honor that truth and find the way to communicate it to a reluctant audience.*

Seriousness

"Life feels like a real fight—as if there were something really wild in the universe which we, with all our idealities and faithfulnesses, are needed to redeem."

—**William James**

"My lifelong ambition has been to unite the utmost seriousness of question with the utmost lightness of form."

—**Milan Kundera**

"A symphony is no joke."

—**Johannes Brahms**

"We are descended not only from monkeys, but also from monks."

—**Elbert Hubbard**

On certain days life seems just too pointless and absurd. But when an artist is engaged with his work—lost in a trance, struggling to understand that portion of the universe he has set himself the task of comprehending—a glorious seriousness pervades the world. To the engaged artist the human predicament is never an empty or frivolous matter: it is a serious spectacle worth his undivided attention.

■ *I am ironic, playful, and cynical—but for all that, I am a serious person. I am lazy, silly, and even cruel—but for all that, I am a serious person. I affirm that I am engaged in fathoming life's secrets: the enigma that is the world, the inexplicable wonder that is art, the riddle that is another human being, and the puzzle that I am myself.*

SHADOWS

The average person is not fond of encountering the shadows dancing in the caverns of her soul or the shadows cast by the million hard objects of the world. But the artist embraces shadows. She travels to shadowy places and returns with her discoveries; she spots the darkness in her neighbor's heart and the darkness in her own heart. This talent does not endear her to others, and in the process she may frighten herself badly. But she never worried much about her popularity and, as to frights, she reckons she has no choice but to risk them.

"The amount of chiaroscuro an idea harbors is the only index of its profundity."

—**E. M. Cioran**

"I'm not interested in the texture of a rock, but in its shadow."

—**Ellsworth Kelly**

"I have a feeling only for shadows."

—**Odilon Redon**

"As is true of many women playwrights, I've not yet delved into the vortex of mother/daughter dynamics. I believe it is the last dark continent to be explored in dramatic material."

—**Kathleen Betsko**

■ *I am inexorably drawn to shadows. When I am among them, my understanding deepens. Let others avoid them: I know that truth is made up of both darkness and light. I will maintain a fine balance, risking encounters with the night but also embracing the airy side of life.*

Simplicity

"Shouldn't it give us pause that the oldest works of art are as impressive today in their beauty and spontaneity as they were many thousands of years ago?"

—Kasimir Malevich

"There is more simplicity in the man who eats caviar on impulse than in the man who eats grape nuts on principle."

—G. K. Chesterton

"Simple pleasures are the last refuge of the complex."

—Oscar Wilde

"With the most primitive means the artist creates something which the most ingenious and efficient technology will never be able to create."

—Kasimir Malevich

To hug a child, to say "Thank you" and mean it, to work several hours at one's art rather than a few, to imbue a single brushstroke with power: these are simple, precious, and unaccountably rare events. How nations relate is a complex matter: must a smile be complex, too? Artists revere the power of simple things, but they have nearly as much trouble as the next person piercing the surface tension under which simple things are mysteriously hidden.

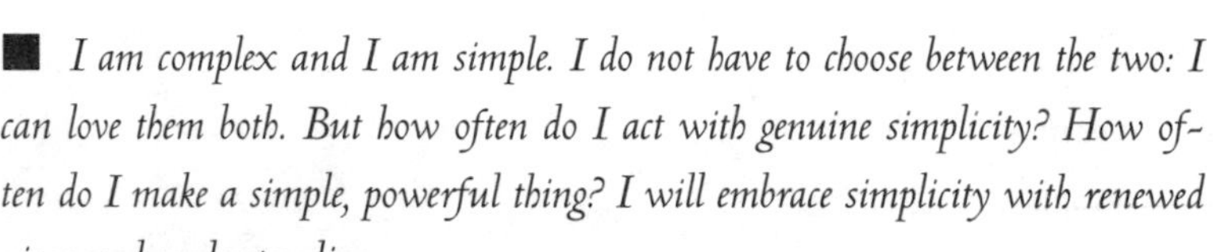

■ *I am complex and I am simple. I do not have to choose between the two: I can love them both. But how often do I act with genuine simplicity? How often do I make a simple, powerful thing? I will embrace simplicity with renewed vigor and understanding.*

SINCERITY

How odd to know that one is both sincere and insincere. But artists acknowledge their dual nature: and that self-knowledge is itself a mark of their fundamental sincerity. The artist by her very nature knows how to manufacture fairy tales, manipulate emotions, exaggerate, falsify, and cast the best light on her subject. She knows how to fashion sound bites and present compelling lies. But she is also aware that she is not exempt from her own self-judgments. If she acts with blithe insincerity, she will find herself hoist with the petard of her own honesty.

"The artist himself may not think he is religious, but if he is sincere his sincerity in itself is religion."

—**EMILY CARR**

"There is an investment of your own life experience in something as innocent as color."

—**STEPHEN DE STAEBLER**

"All that is necessary to paint well is to be sincere."

—**MAURICE DENIS**

"The universe was not made in jest but in solemn incomprehensible earnest."

—**ANNIE DILLARD**

■ *I can tell outrageous lies, work dishonestly, and in a hundred other ways fall short of my ideals. But my dual nature is a richness, if I make sincere use of that dark, insincere, and outrageous part of me. I know what authentic living looks and feels like: I will do an excellent job of manifesting my basic sincerity.*

Society

"Our concern is not how to worship in the catacombs but how to remain human in the skyscrapers."

—**Abraham Heschel**

"Those of us who aren't artists must color things the way they really are or people might think we're stupid."

—**Jules Feiffer**

"The purpose of freedom is to create it for others."

—**Bernard Malamud**

"I live on the fringe of society, and the rules of normal society have no currency for those on the fringe."

—**Tamara de Lempicka**

Whether or not human beings are social animals by nature, they are social animals in fact. They are constrained to resemble the group they are born into, to believe in its gods and values, to walk and talk like their neighbors. The artist, too, is shaped by and must respond to his surroundings: while he would like to work in peace, creating according to his inner lights, he too is a prisoner of his society. He may feel safe in his studio, but it is a false safety: for his society already dwells within him. His society, material for his art, is a whirlwind in his own being.

■ *I have been formed in this time and place: my society is embedded within me. I wish it were otherwise; I wish I had altogether more freedom. But I accept the reality of my situation. I will comprehend the implications of my status as a social animal and make art that speaks to the truth of that understanding.*

Solitude

Solitude is a name we give to communion with self. We are not alone in solitude: we are partnered by our thoughts and dreams. Old friends come, old pains and conundrums, old ruined villas we glimpsed as we wandered the hills of Italy. Solitude is the work space of the artist. In solitude we are silent so that we may hear, focused so that we may craft substantial things. The artist who, craving solitude, achieves it too little, feels sad and cheated: a dozen busy days are no substitute for one rich hour of solitude.

"I love to write out of doors and sleep out of doors, too. If I sleep under the open sky it becomes part of the writing experience, part of my insulation from the world."

—**Margaret Bourke-White**

"Solitude is the furnace of transformation."

—**Henri Nouwen**

"He who does not enjoy solitude will not love freedom."

—**Arthur Schopenhauer**

"I live in that solitude which is painful in youth, but delicious in the years of maturity."

—**Albert Einstein**

■ *I must champion my own solitude. It is absurdly easy to worry myself right out of that sacred state: then I rush off to tend to one thing or another, or become passive and inert. I will not ruin my own solitude: I will protect it, encourage it, love it, and provide ample room for it.*

Space

"Space, and space again, is the infinite deity which surrounds us and in which we are ourselves contained."

—**Max Beckmann**

"We turn clay to make a vessel, but it is on the space where there is nothing that the usefulness of the vessel depends."

—**Lao-tzu**

"In a painting, space doesn't involve practical hazards. You can't break your neck in a painting."

—**Stuart Davis**

"Throw open your window and let the scenery of clouds and sky enter your room!"

—**Yosa Buson**

Because she favors solitude and indwelling, an artist can live a significantly more claustrophobic life than she had ever intended. Life shrinks around her; the four walls of her studio creep inward, reducing her vista. How can she acquire the spaciousness she needs, given her penchant for introspection? Does she need a view of the ocean or of some distant mountains? Would that even help? Or must she consciously open herself—her eyes, her heart, her mind—to the vast space around her?

■ *It is easy to fall into narrow ways; and hard to retain a sense of spaciousness. But I really do prefer the world of breezes, the world of sunlight and fresh ideas, to the world of stuffy air. I can and will do better: I will joyously air out my mind and my work space this very day.*

What does an artist feel? What does she know? To whom can she pray? In what can she believe? She might as well believe in dance: is there something better? She might as well believe in poetry: is there something higher? She might as well believe in film: is there something more magical? She might as well believe in the lullaby she sings her child: is there something nobler? She might as well believe in her own personhood, her own potential: isn't she herself the temple?

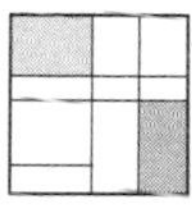

"Music is the electrical soil in which the spirit lives, thinks, and invents."

—LUDWIG VAN BEETHOVEN

"The artist alone sees spirits. But after he has told of their appearing to him, everybody sees them."

—JOHANN WOLFGANG VON GOETHE

"To approach the spiritual in art, one will make as little use as possible of reality, because reality is opposed to the spiritual."

—PIET MONDRIAN

"Rather paint the flying spirit of the bird than its feathers."

—ROBERT HENRI

■ *Without being able to define what I mean, I know that I am a spiritual creature. Something larger than my appetites and desires, finer than my flaws and anxieties, courses through me. But to possess this ineffable spirit is not enough: I must also manifest it through right living and creating.*

SPIRITUALITY

" 'Painting' and 'religious experience' are the same thing."

—**BEN NICHOLSON**

"Making art is the closest I get to God."

—**RHONDA ZWILLINGER**

"Spirituality for me is the sum total of all the acts of my day."

—**ARI GOLDMAN**

"Art thaws even the frozen, darkened soul, opening it to lofty spiritual experience."

—**ALEKSANDR SOLZHENITSYN**

Artists find their clearest understanding of the nature of spirituality revealed to them in the process of creating and performing. They may find something of worth in organized religion or next to nothing, but they know that spiritual fulfillment awaits them in the studio, the practice room, the editing room, the study. The cynical artist and the devout artist are alike in this regard: to each, spirituality and art are one; to each, a world devoid of art would possess the acrid smell of a wasteland.

■ *I will hold the creative process as sacred. If I avoid that process, I am badly diminished. If I engage in it, I experience love and sense the mysterious depths of the universe. Through art I will be fulfilled and revealed; in art I will find the greatest revelations.*

Stamina

An artist's work requires great mental and physical stamina. To memorize the lead in a play or opera, to hold a novel as it runs its course, and to play with vitality the same song for the thousandth time are tasks that can wear down anybody. Isn't an artist's real talent the strength he shows when he revises his story again and again, when he practices diligently for an upcoming audition? Give an artist stamina and you have given him something really valuable.

"When you're in the theater, you work incredibly hard. You must store up your energy for that one burst of light."

—Vera Zorina

"All my life I've wanted to dance the Swan Queen. But I don't know if I could ever do thirty-two *fouettés*."

—Starr Danias

"In everything imposingly beautiful, strength has much to do with the magic."

—Herman Melville

"For anything worth having one must pay the price; and the price is always work, patience, love, and self-sacrifice."

—John Burroughs

■ *I only sometimes have the energy to do my work. My stamina is a fitful thing; for long periods I am unequal to the demands my work makes on me. I dearly need a more constant strength. I will find the optimism, will, and mental health that together will raise my stamina level.*

STARDOM

"I was always emotionally disturbed that I was not a star. My self-image was that I was better than any comedian who ever lived, and I was sick enough to believe it. It was a constant, compulsive, overriding, overwhelming need."

—**Jackie Mason**

"Legends are fine if you've got somebody who loves you, some man who's not afraid to be in love with Judy Garland."

—**Judy Garland**

"I never wanted to be a star. I don't even like the attention of a birthday party."

—**Joni Mitchell**

"Success has made failures of many men."

—**Cindy Adams**

Stardom is bad for everyone. It alienates the millions of working artists who don't achieve it and plays havoc with the few who do. Ideally, every artist would speak and be heard, would work and be paid, would find and inhabit a niche in the culture. In reality, most artists live and work in obscurity, out of place and out of sorts, while the luminaries they envy hire bodyguards and wonder what their friends are about to divulge to the *National Enquirer.*

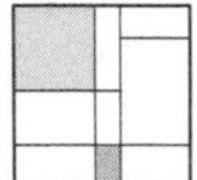

■ *I recognize that I crave stardom. How can I best deal with this heartbreaking burden? The greatest challenge I face might be exactly this: to find a way to feel fulfilled, whether or not I achieve stardom.*

Many, if not most, artists have trouble starting. It is not the journey that daunts them so much as the packing for the journey; not the writing of the song, but the packing away of untidy doubts, fears, and self-recriminations. So a year goes by and nothing new gets started. Littered all around are the clothes that, if folded, would fit nicely into the suitcase: but all the artist is able to see are messy reproaches. Let her just pick up one single sock and fold it!

"It is sad that my emotional dependence on the man I love should have killed so much of my energy and ability; there was certainly once a great deal of energy in me."

—**Sonya Tolstoy**

"All large tasks are completed in a series of starts."

—**Neil Fiore**

"Better by far to write twaddle or anything, anything, than nothing at all."

—**Katherine Mansfield**

"The reason why worry kills more people than work is that more people worry than work."

—**Robert Frost**

■ *When I grit my teeth and wage war with myself, I rarely start. But when I take a good, deep breath and surrender to what will be, I start easily. Then I have accomplished the artist's miracle: doing the small thing that adds up finally to a great summation. I will start: I will fearlessly and quietly tackle whatever wants doing.*

Stillness

"If they try to rush me, I always say, 'I've only got one other speed—and it's slower.' "

—**Glenn Ford**

"Everybody gets so much information all day long that they lose their common sense."

—**Gertrude Stein**

"I tend to move toward still points."

—**Joan Didion**

"There are wonderful moments, those rare moments when there is silence, a tangible silence out there, a silence deeper than silence."

—**Derek Jacobi**

Like a meditation master, like a thoughtful, reflective person in any walk of life, the artist reveres stillness. He recognizes that the silences between the notes make the music; he understands how out of a deep calm rise tempestuous bursts of creativity. But if an artist becomes too harried and busy, too unsettled and unhappy, the stillness he reveres will desert him. Recalling the joy that stillness brings, he must then find ways to encourage the return of that certain silence.

■ *In the stillness that I love I am never bored, never alone, never worried. In that calm, I am the artist I was meant to be. I must create that stillness for myself, I must woo it and nurture it: I will make the quiet I need.*

Stubbornness

Does an artist pop out of the womb with a gift for obstinacy? Does she look up at her parents and in that first split second decide, "I'm going to butt heads with these people"? It is entirely possible that an artist is born stubborn; and of course that stubbornness will get her into trouble. Still, it is a gift, for she needs to be obstinate in order to survive the life she has chosen. How, after all, can she direct herself, trust herself, or take care of herself unless she is really adamant?

"I begin to feel an enormous need to become savage and to create a new world."
—**Paul Gauguin**

"I don't think I will mellow out. It is not in my blood."
—**Van Morrison**

"For a girl without a self, I was pretty stubborn."
—**Eleanor Antin**

"Ye shall know the truth, and the truth shall make you mad."
—**Aldous Huxley**

■ *I must be stubborn enough to survive, but not so stubborn as to refuse to adapt; I must learn when and how to hold the line, budge an inch, or budge a mile. I affirm that I am stubborn—but not foolishly stubborn—and that I will learn which stubbornness is which.*

Study

"I know that the twelve notes in each octave and the varieties of rhythm offer me opportunities that all human genius will never exhaust."

—**Igor Stravinsky**

"No art was ever less spontaneous than mine. What I do is the result of reflection and study."

—**Edgar Degas**

"The best advice I can give to a young actor is this: Learn your lines."

—**Spencer Tracy**

"When you see somebody dead for the first time, you can't resist making notes on the way you yourself feel, to use when poignancy is called for."

—**John Gielgud**

When an artist really studies his medium, it shows: you sense the thousand movies he's loved in the one he's made, hear something of the thousand songs he's hummed in the one he's recorded. The elegant conclusion to his story is the result of the sweat he's poured into countless unsuccessful lines; his briefest sketch is informed by his decades of study. Artists study because it is their duty and because they love to do it.

■ *A lifelong study of the materials and methods of my discipline is vital to my success as an artist. Art is research as well as spontaneous action, scholarship as well as imagination. I will study more: I affirm my sincere love for the past, present, and future of my medium.*

Subjectivity

To memorize a score, to work out the fingerings, to play as fast and as slow as the piece demands is already a great deal. But still that will get the performer only a string of dead notes. Until she pours her heart into her work and risks her own subjective interpretation, an artist hasn't made art. What is an objective painting? An objective novel? An objective interpretation of a script or song? The artist who denies or attempts to minimize his part in his art only announces that he is a human being in hiding.

"That your own interpretation of a work of art is flagrantly subjective seems to be regarded as an arrogant attitude. But the truer view is that the interpretative artist can only make his own comment upon the work."

—Tyrone Guthrie

"Since the last decades of the nineteenth century, revolt against the objectified world has determined the character of art and literature."

—Paul Tillich

"Art pierces opaque subjectivity, the *not* seeing of conventional life, and discloses reality."

—Langdon Gilkey

"Content is a glimpse."

—Willem de Kooning

■ *I will interpret life as I see and feel it. Even as I respect the texts I use, I will bring my own subjective stamp to them. I will infuse my creative work with my being; and accept that the finished work then reveals me and reflects on me. I am not only objective: I am a fully subjective artist.*

SUCCESS

"The common idea that success spoils people by making them vain, egotistic, and self-complacent is erroneous; on the contrary, it makes them, for the most part, humble, tolerant, and kind.

—**W. Somerset Maugham**

"Success didn't spoil me; I've always been insufferable."

—**Fran Lebowitz**

"The toughest thing about success is that you've got to keep on being a success."

—**Irving Berlin**

"I'd like to live like a poor man with lots of money."

—**Pablo Picasso**

Does the successful, well-known artist feel obliged to act humanely toward his peers, mentoring and encouraging them? Or does he sneer at them and disparage them instead? Presumably he understands that he is one of the very lucky ones, an exception to the rule; if he heeds the call of his conscience he is bound to show some real generosity. But how many successful artists in fact heed the call of conscience? Whatever the number, it ought to be larger.

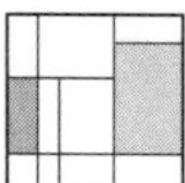

■ *I mean to be successful. I do not fear success; I have no doubts whatsoever that I really want it. I will be improved by my success, rather than ruined by it: I affirm that I will be a model star, dignified, compassionate, and helpful. I will be someone who deserves it.*

Suffering

Suffering is unavoidable. Wise artists neither glorify suffering nor hope to inoculate themselves against it, but rather affirm that they will remain empathic witnesses to the suffering. Open and vulnerable, they allow suffering to enrich and transform their life and their work. If they must write about death, they suffer but still sit down to write; if they must challenge their times, they suffer the scorn and rejection without responding with hate. They brave the suffering and heroically remain adamant, human, and loving, artists to the end.

"If suffering alone taught, all the world would be wise. To suffering must be added mourning, understanding, patience, love, openness, and the willingness to remain vulnerable."

—Anne Morrow Lindbergh

"Only life suffered can transform a symphony from a collection of notes into a message of humanity."

—Dimitri Mitropoulos

"The artist is the child in the popular fable, every one of whose tears was a pearl."

—Heinrich Heine

"Every man, on the foundation of his sufferings and joys, builds for all."

—Albert Camus

■ *Since my goal is not ease but authentic living, I can suffer and still fulfill my destiny. I would prefer not to suffer, and I offer it no standing invitation: but I will not take safe detours just because I fear that on the risky path I may suffer.*

SURVIVAL

"Actors are a much hardier breed of people than any other people. We have to be as clever as rats to survive."

—**Maureen Stapleton**

"Always be smarter than the people who hire you."

—**Lena Horne**

"The teacher tortured me. Whether he recognized that my desire to study was serious and sincere, or whether he saw in me a defenseless and willing victim, I do not know."

—**Odilon Redon**

"Tell me, on your soul and conscience, do you believe that anything of mine will live?"

—**Alexandre Dumas Père**

How clever an artist must be just to survive! And how little the notion of "survival skills" captures the amazing resilience and fortitude an artist must possess in order to make a living, do creative work, and safeguard his mental health. How will an aging rock-and-roller keep selling records to children? What will motivate a painter to start a new painting when he surveys his studio and sees a hundred unsold ones? How long can an actor live on a day job and the occasional industrial commercial? But all of this and more an artist must survive: which makes survival an artist's full-time business.

■ *Don't pay me. Don't call me. Don't want me. Criticize me. Reject me. Tell me that the arts are not needed or that there are too many artists. Tell me to get a real job. Tell me to grow up. Tell me that my work is ugly. Tell me that my former classmate is a star now. Do or say anything: I will survive—and even find my own way of thriving.*

Talent is one of those indefinable, worshiped words. A pianist's talent may involve his depth of character much more than his manual dexterity; the singer who loves to sing may improve her sound by her loving attitude. Is the talented writer the one who knows the rules of grammar or the one who adores language? May a painter's talent consist mainly in painting against all odds for two decades? Talent is so loaded a word, so full to the brim with meanings, that an artist might be wise to forget about it altogether and just keep on working.

"A lot of hogwash is talked about acting. It's not all that fancy! You laugh, you cry, you pick up a little bit, and then you're a working actor."

—**KATHARINE HEPBURN**

"I have once more taken up things that can't be done: water with grasses weaving on the bottom. But I'm always tackling that sort of thing!"

—**CLAUDE MONET**

"It must be a sign of talent that I do not give up, though I can get nobody to take an interest in my efforts."

—**FANNY MENDELSSOHN HENSEL**

"There are only 1,500 musicians of world class on this planet, and they must be handled with care and respect."

—**ERNEST FLEISCHMANN**

■ *I am talented. That means above all else that I must work hard, for talent is a muscle; if I exercise that muscle, my art will grow strong. I prize the ability to draw a circle freehand or to sing on key, but such skills are only a part of my talent: my greatest talent is in fully exercising my humanity.*

TEAMWORK

"The choreographer's own work is difficult and nerve-racking enough and he doesn't want a girl who sulks, has hysterics, or starts quarrels in the company."

—**AGNES DE MILLE**

"In the production of a good play with a good cast and a knowing director there is formed a fraternity whose members share a mutual sense of destiny."

—**ARTHUR MILLER**

"People who make music together cannot be enemies, at least not while the music lasts."

—**PAUL HINDEMITH**

"People must never be humiliated—that is the chief thing."

—**ANTON CHEKHOV**

How often do the members of a band or orchestra, the many hands involved in the making of a play, book, or movie, the scores of souls involved in mounting the new opera or ethnic dance festival experience the joys of teamwork? All too rarely. But the conclusion for an artist to draw is not that teamwork is impossible, but rather that team building is one of her vital jobs: that she has an enduring part to play in the construction of meaningful relationships.

■ *I may not have been born a team player, but I understand the necessity of teamwork in art. I will treat my fellow team members with respect and demand respect in return. I have excellent reasons to join with others; I will provide others with excellent reasons to want to join with me.*

TREACHERY

Lost in private work, feeling pressured to excel and driven to succeed, careless about relationships, and a law unto himself, an artist is in danger of acting treacherously toward others. Will he sculpt a satiric bust, not minding that he is hurting a friend's feelings? Forget that his mate has been waiting for hours to chat with him? Rudely dismiss his children, on the grounds that his new song needs his undivided attention? An artist who is too self-centered is liable to exhibit faults he abhors: carelessness, callousness, and even downright cruelty.

"I'm basically a treacherous person with no sense of loyalty. I'd write openly about my sainted mother's sex life for art."

—**SUSAN BRAUDY**

"We are more often treacherous through weakness than through calculation."

—**LA ROCHEFOUCAULD**

"Writers are always selling somebody out."

—**JOAN DIDION**

"I am not sincere, not even when I say I am not."

—**JULES RENARD**

■ *I will not be a treacherous person. I have committed acts of treachery in the past; the possibility for future treachery resides within me. But I will do better: I will care more about others and treat them fairly, for their own sake and for mine as well.*

TRUST

"An artist, under pain of oblivion, must have confidence in himself."

—**Pierre-Auguste Renoir**

"Never, even as a child, would I bend to a rule."

—**Claude Monet**

"My paintings are not about what is seen. They are about what is known forever in the mind."

—**Agnes Martin**

"I think that we may safely trust a good deal more than we do."

—**Henry David Thoreau**

Why would an artist not trust himself? Because in his own estimation he feels untrustworthy. He wants to trust his memory but forgets his lines. He wants to trust his judgment but ruins his painting with a single stroke. He wants to trust his skills but writes a play that stinks up the studio. The answer to this terrible dilemma is twofold: an artist must trust himself completely, even if he isn't worthy of that trust quite yet; and he must earn his own trust over time, by working well and growing in artistry.

■ *To be successful, I must trust myself. To trust myself, I must succeed at my work and honor my successes. I will solve this chicken-and-egg dilemma by both trusting myself right now and succeeding as an artist. I am worthy of my own sacred trust; and I will grow worthier.*

TRUTH

There exists a perennial coffee house debate: "There is truth!" "No, there's not!" "This is a truth!" "No, that's just a fact!" "Well, then, this is a truth!" "No, that's just true by definition!" "Well, truth isn't just relative!" "Yes, it is!" "No, it isn't!" The wise artist avoids standing on the sidelines in this fashion, unengaged and deeply idle. Instead he affirms that he has true work to do, whether or not "the truth" is a viable philosophical entity; he affirms his own true work, and does it.

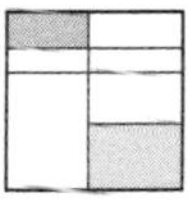

"All my thinking about art is haunted by a mystical belief that in its practice one is tapping sources of truth."

—**Roger Hilton**

"The truth is more important than the facts."

—**Frank Lloyd Wright**

"There is a tragic clash between Truth and the world. Pure undistorted truth burns up the world."

—**Nikolai Berdyaev**

"Truth exists. Only lies are invented."

—**Georges Braque**

■ *Upholding truth is my lifelong work. As elusive as the truth may be, it comes clear for a moment when I work deeply and honorably. I affirm my allegiance to the truth: whatever it is, however it shifts, and whatever discomfort I feel in not really comprehending it.*

Truth-Telling

"Certainly, audiences have flocked to see films that are not essentially true, but I don't think this prevents them from responding to the truth."

—**Stanley Kubrick**

"It does not require many words to speak the truth."

—**Chief Joseph**

"I care about truth, not for truth's sake but for my own."

—**Samuel Butler**

"Each man insists on being innocent, even if it means accusing the whole human race, and heaven."

—**Albert Camus**

Hard truths are discouraging and subversive, for they remind us of reality and show us the chinks in the status quo. The telling of these hard truths, in psychological novels, jarring paintings, or searing dramas, inevitably puts truth-tellers in jeopardy. Today artists are dismissed, and not drawn and quartered; ignored, and not immolated. But even as they are spared the death penalty, they are subject to profound consequences as a result of their truth-telling. Isn't the shunned artist suffering a real punishment?

■ *As an artist, I will withhold the truth when I must and tell the truth when I must, according to my understanding of what is humane and just in a given situation. I am a truth-teller: I willingly accept the dangers that come with honest speaking.*

UGLINESS

The ugly tickles and prickles the artist. When his beautiful pot sags and commas clog up his sentences, it is his nemesis. But it is his dear friend when, to make a point about mere beauty, he asserts that ugliness is his only real subject matter. He matches ugly colors to wake up the dead, then weeps when he sees that the colors he chose were really just too ugly. Ugliness! The strange, unbeautiful face beautiful in its ugliness; the perfect, beautiful face ugly in its perfection. Ugliness! The artist's grist and gristle.

"Nothing's beautiful from every point of view."

—HORACE

"What makes sovereign ugliness are our conventions."

—EUGÈNE DELACROIX

"Frequently in nature, trees will be found to be ugly in shape. As an artist, whose purpose is to create things of beauty, why not change such ugly features?"

—FRANK RINES

"It's better to say, 'I'm suffering,' than to say, 'This landscape is ugly.' "

—W. H. AUDEN

■ *I accept the shifting senses of ugliness. If I am a standard-bearer for truth, goodness, and beauty, I must also defend the ugly: for my own ugly work may be the ashes out of which my next great work rises. I will champion ugliness: not for its own sake, but because it is inexorably a part of the fabric I am weaving.*

Understanding

"Real painters understand with a brush in their hand."

—**Berthe Morisot**

"It is difficult to get a man to understand something when his salary depends upon his not understanding it."

—**Upton Sinclair**

"It is a luxury to be understood."

—**Ralph Waldo Emerson**

"Talking about things that are understandable only weighs down the mind."

—**Alfred Jarry**

Artists get only glimmers of understanding. At first, with the arrogance of youth, they imagine that they understand everything; but by their fourth movie, their twentieth mural, their hundredth poem, they begin to see that incomplete understanding is a feature of the human condition. They see how they themselves are implicated in their lack of understanding: how their thoughts drift, their eyes blur, their hands tire. The wise artist makes peace with the fact that he will understand less than he had anticipated: makes his peace, sheds some bitter tears, and still holds out for more.

■ *I am sad that I understand as little as I do. But I will not be defeated by this human fact. I will study, make fine connections, and increase what I know drop by drop. What I do understand, I will make understandable to others: through my art, our mutual understanding will grow.*

VIBRATIONS

This is not a culture that puts much stock in subtle vibrations, in the resonance of a chant or the feel of a jagged rock. The artist who pictures sounds as colors, who feels the difference in microns between one sea green and another, who senses a mighty theme in a seashell's shape, is not attending to what the world considers important. But off the artist drifts, caught in the undertows of meaning that swirl around her, moved by unseen currents.

"The key of D is daffodil yellow, B major is maroon, and B flat is blue."

—MARIAN MCPARTLAND

"What happens to the hole when the cheese is gone?"

—BERTOLT BRECHT

"I don't express myself in my paintings. I express my not-self."

—MARK ROTHKO

"I pick up a small, brown pebble because I want to experience it. The stone is throbbing to the slow rhythms of geologic time, a vibration I can only imagine because it is below the threshold of human perception."

—ESTHER WARNER DENDEL

■ *Even if I'm gawked at as I measure nothing with great diligence, even if I perplex myself as I pick up stray radiation from the universe, still I affirm my love affair with life's invisible vibrations. As an artist, I will hear what is not said and see what is left out of the picture.*

VULNERABILITY

"I had always functioned with dignity, wanting to appear intelligent, macho, never vulnerable or insecure. But now I realize that the dumbness that is so much a part of these comic characters is a fundamental part of me, too."

—**LESLIE NIELSEN**

"Acting is standing up naked and turning around very slowly."

—**ROSALIND RUSSELL**

"Misfortunes one can endure. But to suffer for one's own faults—ah!—there is the sting of life."

—**OSCAR WILDE**

"Tell me that not everything I wrote was bad."

—**MAURICE RAVEL**

How vulnerable we feel when we confront our flaws, determine to steer a new course in the marketplace, or accept the reality of another person. Artists, who already risk wounding as they audition or submit their poems, have their books reviewed, or have the slides of their paintings scrutinized, must risk even more if they are to find love and successes. An artist feels vulnerable to begin with; and yet the only answer is to recklessly discard more armor.

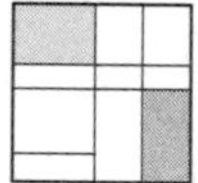

■ *How open and vulnerable can I manage to be? I can't love if I erect a wall between myself and another. I can't create if I flee from real encounters with chaos. I can't compete in the marketplace if I refuse to show my work. It appears I have no choice: I must risk feeling vulnerable a million times over.*

Who Am I?

Artists must stop sometimes and take stock. Is pursuing live theater still the right choice, given all that an artist has learned after years in the trenches? Should she try her hand at nonfiction now, rather than rush into the writing of her seventh novel? Who is the artist today? Is she the same person she was at twenty? Has she the same needs, the same dreams, the same aspirations? How can she know unless she pauses and asks herself questions?

"What are you? What am I? Those are the questions that constantly persecute and torment me and perhaps also play some part in my art."

—**Max Beckmann**

"A man shows reckless courage in entering into the abyss of himself."

—**William Butler Yeats**

"Self-acquaintance is a rare condition."

—**Robert Henri**

"Life must be lived forwards. But it must be understood backwards."

—**Søren Kierkegaard**

■ *I will risk understanding myself. This is a real risk, anxiety-provoking, hard on my ego, and an invitation to pain. I may have to reevaluate my goals and chart for myself a new course of action. Still, I will know myself. I affirm my commitment to self-knowledge.*

WHOLENESS

"In every painting a whole is mysteriously enclosed, a whole life of tortures, doubts, of hours of enthusiasm and inspiration."

—**WASSILY KANDINSKY**

"When you look up at the sky, you have a feeling of unity which delights you and makes you giddy."

—**FERDINAND HODLER**

"For the artist what and how are one."

—**WILLIAM MCELCHERAN**

"Open your eyes! The world is still intact."

—**PAUL CLAUDEL**

A painting is not meaningfully defined by cataloging the wavelengths of the pigments employed. Nor is a person meaningfully defined by summing up her virtues and vices, her two hundred poems, her five hundred concerts, or the million moments she has managed to survive. Wholeness is not like anything else: a whole is a different truth. While some part of the artwork may fail, the whole may have its own unique importance; and while the artist may despair about her particulars, she can consider herself a wonder to behold in her entirety.

■ *If I dwell on a single painful feeling or unfortunate fact, I can lose hope. I must keep my eye on the whole panorama, where grandeur resides. I affirm that wholeness is a triumph and a reality; and that I myself can be whole.*

Will

Can a person grow willpower as he would muscles? Or is he limited to the willpower he's so far shown? The wise artist assumes the former: he assumes that his lack of willpower, as demonstrated by blocks and bad habits, proves nothing about tomorrow. Tomorrow he may flip a switch and become mobilized. Tomorrow the experiences he's accumulated may translate into amazing horsepower. Tomorrow he may recover from the troubles of his childhood. Tomorrow—or today—he may love himself better and work harder.

"You create your own propulsion for going onstage each night."

—**Anthony Quinn**

"There are a million people who can come up with little bits. The hard work is making those bits into something."

—**Jeff Lynne**

"There is no love where there is no will."

—**Mohandas K. Gandhi**

"My mountain is dead. As soon as she has dried, I'll bury her under a decent layer of white paint. But I haven't done with the old lady; far from it!"

—**Emily Carr**

■ *I am willing. I have strength, endurance, stamina. Do I manifest that willpower enough? No. Can I manifest it more? Yes! I will do my work right now, again tomorrow, and then again the day after.*

Witnessing

"We act as though it were our mission to bring about the triumph of truth, but our mission is only to fight for it."

—**Blaise Pascal**

"I shall not weary of testifying. I consider myself responsible to the coming generations, which are left stranded in a blitzed world, unaware of the soul trembling in awe before the mystery of life."

—**Oskar Kokoschka**

"The artist has to be a guardian of the culture."

—**Robert Longo**

"Artists have to show us what is not going well within the person and within the society, not try to cover it up."

—**Thich Nhat Hanh**

The artist harbors the silly, splendid notion that she can save the world. Somehow she will save it from injustice, intolerance, meanness, and pain; from human folly, human hatred, even from human nature. She can't, of course; but her passionate engagement amounts to a kind of salvation. She saves herself from the charge of inauthentic living, and by witnessing and reporting, she does her singular part to keep civilization from crumbling.

■ *I tremble before what I see: but I will see it. I am disturbed by what I see: but I will bear witness. My heart is wounded by what I see: but I will look right at it. I will communicate what I see to others, in any medium I can make sing. Why? Because my humanity demands it.*

Work

Even the work an artist most loves to do is still part drudgery. Even work an artist dreams of engaging in—a large movie, an electric band, an exceptional dance season, a right-feeling novel—is still a matter of aching limbs and dull paragraphs, band squabbles and last-minute script revisions. The wise, productive artist recognizes this and *still* works, making sure not to use as an excuse the truth that art-making is not sheer play. Creativity is part sweat—not just beads of it, but sometimes buckets.

"The best part of one's life is the working part."

—Garson Kanin

"Without work all life goes rotten."

—Albert Camus

"The great man is sparing in words but prodigal in deeds."

—Confucius

"The best way out is always through."

—Robert Frost

"It is by acts and not by ideas that people live."

—Anatole France

■ *I have a vast amount of work to do. Can an opera come into being without real work? Can a novel? Can I compress the universe into a poem without some struggle? I will work; I must work. I affirm that I will start each day on a work trajectory.*

WORKAHOLISM

"If I hadn't been at work all the time, I would have been a lunatic."

—INGMAR BERGMAN

"I have to keep working. Vacations are not good for me. When I work I'm straight."

—ROBERT ENGMAN

"Work is my norm. I have mad energy, insane energy, a kind of stamina in terms of work that's a little crazy."

—SIDNEY LUMET

"One's real life is often the life that one does not lead."

—OSCAR WILDE

What's an artist to do if he's constantly brimming over with ideas? If he's obsessed and feels compelled to work? What arguments can he manufacture to convince himself that he should shut his engine off? How can he prevent himself from attacking all the blank canvas in the world? Or should he do nothing but work and work? No, of course not: he really must stop sometimes. For there is too much love lost in all this obsessing; a balanced life lost in this driven, daredevil productivity.

■ *I must work. I love taking an idea to completion, writing songs, making movies, sculpting stone, playing jazz till morning. This love is not a problem. But I affirm that there are other sacred tasks—such as being a friend, loving my mate and children, participating in good causes—that require their own full measure of time and attention.*

Yes-Saying

The artist says "No!" to dogma and injustice. She says "No!" to those who doubt the value of art and the immensity of human potential. But when does she say "Yes!"? Will her great yes-saying come in the context of art-making? Will she say yes to family and friends, to good causes and fine adventures, to a lifetime of learning and effort? To keep her spirits up and to preserve her mental health, she needs a host of yes-saying occasions: for every obstinate "No!" a joyous "Yes!" is needed.

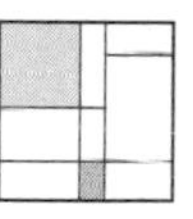

"The anarchist painter is not the one who will create anarchist pictures, but the one who will fight with all his individuality against official conventions."

—**Paul Signac**

"If I lived my life like I play my drums, I wouldn't have any problems."

—**Tony Williams**

"I don't want to represent man as he is, but only as he might be."

—**Albert Camus**

"Beauty is the love that we devote to an object."

—**Paul Sérusier**

With my life and my art I will manage great yes-saying. I will affirm my work, my relationships, and my world; and I will affirm myself. I am an artist, which phrase is itself a terrific affirmation.

Afterword

I would love to hear your thoughts about this book or about your experiences as an artist. You can call me at (925) 689-0210, fax me at the same number, or write to me at the following address:

Dr. Eric Maisel
P.O. Box 613
Concord, CA 94522-0613

For a fuller treatment of the challenges artists face with regard to their personality, work, and world, I invite you to examine a previous book of mine, *A Life in the Arts.* A second book, *Fearless Creating,* offers an in-depth look at the creative process and work-related issues. Both are available from Tarcher/Putnam (to order, call 1-800-788-6262). You may also want to visit my website at www.ericmaisel.com. I also offer a free monthly creativity newsletter. To subscribe to it you can visit my website or send an e-mail directly to creativitynewsletter-subscribe@egroups.com. Thanks! I hope you find these to be valuable resources.

INDEX

ACHIEVING BALANCE

AN ARTIST'S HAPPINESS

CAREER

CULTIVATING INNER ART DISCIPLINES

CULTIVATING QUALITIES

EMOTIONS

MYSTERY

NECESSARY RISKS

NURTURING SELF

PSYCHOLOGICAL CHALLENGES

RELATIONSHIPS

TRAPS

TRUTH, BEAUTY, AND GOODNESS

WORKING